ARLINGTON HEIGHTS
ILLINOIS

Gerry & Janet Souter

ARLINGTON HEIGHTS
ILLINOIS

A BRIEF HISTORY

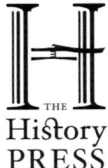

THE
History
PRESS

Published by The History Press
Charleston, SC 29403
www.historypress.net

Copyright © 2009 by Gerry and Janet Souter
All rights reserved

First published 2009

Manufactured in the United States

ISBN 978.1.59629.674.9

Library of Congress Cataloging-in-Publication Data

Souter, Gerry.
Arlington Heights, Illinois : a brief history / Gerry and Janet Souter.
p. cm.
Includes bibliographical references and index.
ISBN 978-1-59629-674-9 (alk. paper)
1. Arlington Heights (Ill.)--History. I. Souter, Janet, 1940- II. Title.
F549.A67S58 2009
977.3'1--dc22
2009017634

Notice: The information in this book is true and complete to the best of our knowledge. It is offered without guarantee on the part of the authors or The History Press. The authors and The History Press disclaim all liability in connection with the use of this book.

All rights reserved. No part of this book may be reproduced or transmitted in any form whatsoever without prior written permission from the publisher except in the case of brief quotations embodied in critical articles and reviews.

*To Cynthia Clampitt,
a caring colleague and insightful author*

CONTENTS

	Acknowledgements	9
Chapter 1	Wagon Ruts Over Pottawatomie Trails	11
Chapter 2	Growing Up by the Tracks	25
Chapter 3	Education and Worship Come to Arlington Heights	43
Chapter 4	Fire, Police and Plumbing	49
Chapter 5	Arlington Heights Marches Off to War	57
Chapter 6	Prohibition—The Beginning and End in 1919	65
Chapter 7	Pulling Together through the Great Depression	75
Chapter 8	Arlington Heights on the Homefront	85
Chapter 9	Baby Boom and Building Boom	95
Chapter 10	Downtown Way Down—1960s Arlington Heights	103
Chapter 11	Protection and Prevention Grow with the Village	115
Chapter 12	Construction and Destruction Go Hand in Hand	121
Chapter 13	Arlington Heights Reinvents Itself	131
Chapter 14	No Conclusion in Sight	149
	Notes	151
	Bibliography	155
	About the Authors	157
	About the Artist	159

ACKNOWLEDGEMENTS

The authors would like to thank the following residents of Arlington Heights, Illinois, for their gracious cooperation and willingness to share valuable memories of village life over the decades. To appreciate our community, its history must be shared through scrapbooks and picture albums, diaries and correspondence, well-worn artifacts lovingly preserved. We visited many homes and individuals who carefully presented family treasures to us either as stories or as images and objects we held in our hands. To all our Arlington Heights neighbors we owe a debt of gratitude: Glenn Adams, Shirley Brown, Jerry Beauvais, Matthew Bennett, Don Dattilo, Dick Bokelman, Margery Frisbie, Bob Frisk, Jodee Lohr Gieseke, LeVern and Glenn Gieseke, Mickey Horndasch, Bill Kruser, Nancy Kluz, Debbie Kuehne, Lloyd Meyer, Dr. Robert Muench, Mayor Arlene Mulder, Val Novak, Catherine Quigg, Janet Brown McCarthy, James Murray, Jack Musich, Scott Shirley, Donna Turek, Pat Gieseke Winkelman and David Zenner.

Chapter 1

WAGON RUTS OVER POTTAWATOMIE TRAILS

Many early settlers who arrived at the bottom swell of Lake Michigan's shore about the year 1818 most likely expected a silent wilderness. If so, they were disappointed. The tract of land named Illinois after the Illiniwek tribes that ranged along its waterways had just become one of the United States of America, and it was booming. The explorers Father Pierre Marquette and Louis Joliet had long ago passed this way in 1673 and used the mile-and-a-half-long slough called the *Chicago Portage* to carry their canoes and equipment overland, shortening their trek from the Des Plaines River to the South Branch of the Chicago River where it emptied into Lake Michigan. The swampy beach that stank of wild onions (*Checagou*) was a strategic location for a trading center.

By the time Illinois became a state, three wars had been fought over its ground: the British against the French, ending in 1763; George Rogers Clark and his defeat of British Forts Kaskaskia and Vincennes in 1778–79; and the American army against the British and their Native American allies during the War of 1812. That year, Chicago became a key outpost when the U.S. government chose to invade Canada as retribution against British persecution of American trade vessels at sea.

Fort Dearborn had been built on the shore of the Chicago River. Settlers and traders in the area flocked to the fort as Pottawatomie Indians, stirred up by the British, attacked in marauding bands. A detachment of Miami Indians allied to the United States and commanded by Captain William Wells arrived in time to escort the soldiers and civilians from the surrounded fort. As the column of men, women and children followed a trail along the lakefront beach south from the fort, Wells became aware that the Pottawatomie—surly because they had been denied plunder and a good fight—had surrounded his party. At about today's Eighteenth Street and Chicago's lakefront, in a

Arlington Heights, Illinois

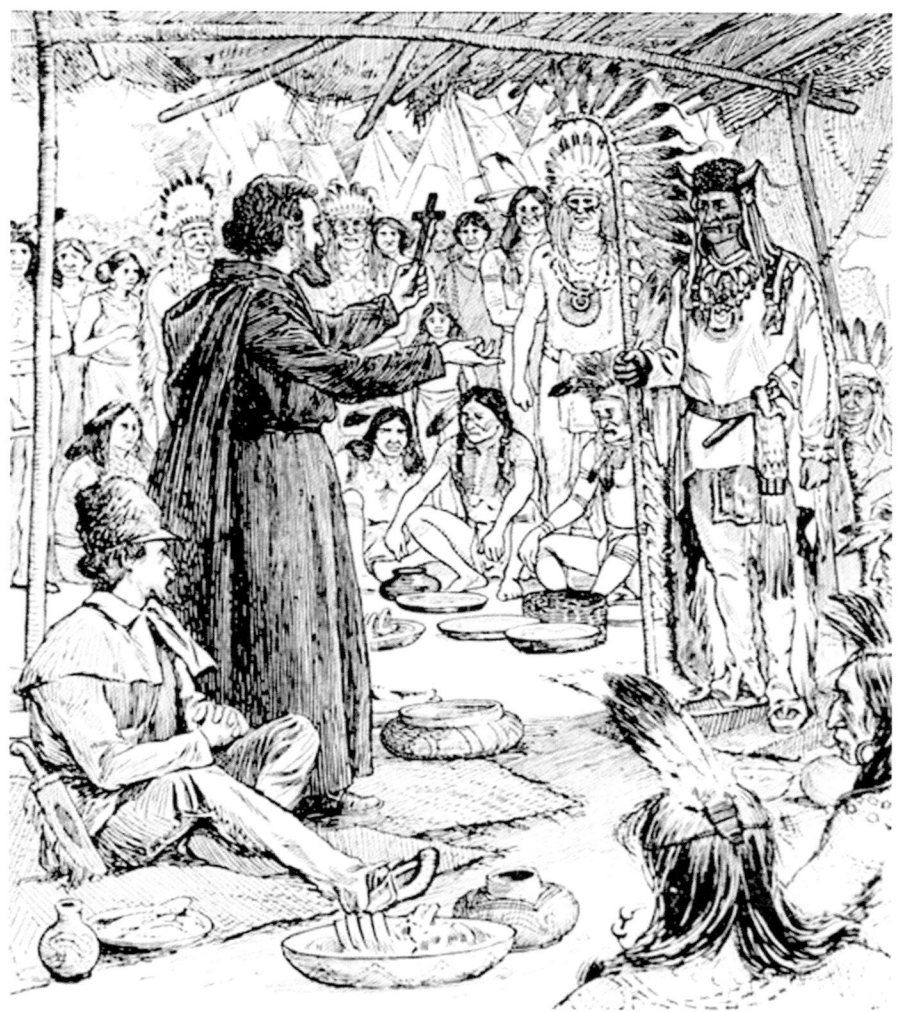

In the late 1600s, explorers Father Louis Joliet and Father Pere Marquette speak to a gathering of Native Americans in the territory that became Illinois. *Courtesy of the Library of Congress.*

masterpiece of questionable judgment, Wells began to curse and berate the growing mob of hostiles, demanding safe passage as promised. This upset the Pottawatomies, who pulled him off his horse, carved open his chest and ate his still-beating heart. They then began slaughtering everyone they could lay hands upon. Of the ninety-three who followed Wells, thirty-eight soldiers, two women and twelve children were slain in the fifteen-minute massacre. Survivors were roped together and marched off to the British as slaves.[1]

Wagon Ruts Over Pottawatomie Trails

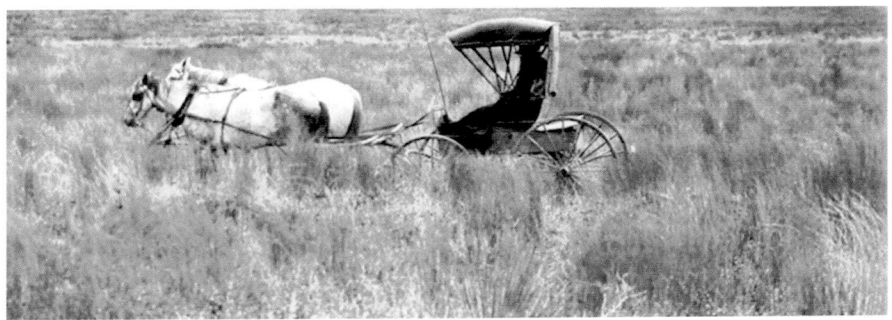

This is how the Midwestern prairie appeared in the 1830s when Asa Dunton purchased the land that is now Arlington Heights. *Courtesy of the National Archives.*

Following that War of 1812–14, sailing ships peacefully plied the Great Lakes and riverboats made their way up and down the Mississippi and Illinois Rivers by oar, sail and pole. These vessels brought lumber from the northern forests, iron and tinware from eastern forges and bolts of cloth from southern textile mills. Dirt roads crisscrossed the prairie, widened out from Native American footpaths and deer trails that followed the contours of the rolling land that had been shaped by the retreat of ancient glaciers.

Many of those rolling hills were man-made by prehistoric mound-building tribes who established the first villages and semi-permanent settlements, the Hopewell and Mississippian Cultures, who left behind only fragmentary artifacts and glimpses of their vanished lifestyle. Farmers and immigrants from the East leveled many of those sacred mounds to grow crops and build homes. In northwest Illinois, the Native American tribes—whole interlocking nations—were pushed west, first in 1832 by the Blackhawk War against that chief and his people and then by the Treaty of Chicago in 1833 that displaced the thousands of Pottawatomie. The Native Americans could hunt on the land, but it no longer belonged to them. The concept of "owning" land was foreign to the Native American peoples, who considered themselves *part* of the land.

Yankees who felt constrained by the overpopulated East and overworked soil moved west behind horses and oxen. One of these families was headed by Asa Dunton, a stone cutter by trade, from Oswego, New York, who purchased three 160-acre parcels of land for himself and his two sons. He, his wife Lois Hawkes and their brood of children arrived at their boundary stakes in 1837. By this time, the "Redskins" had virtually disappeared except for the occasional hunting camp, but their signature remained on the land as their hunting trails became rutted by the wheels of passing wagons. The

Arlington Heights, Illinois

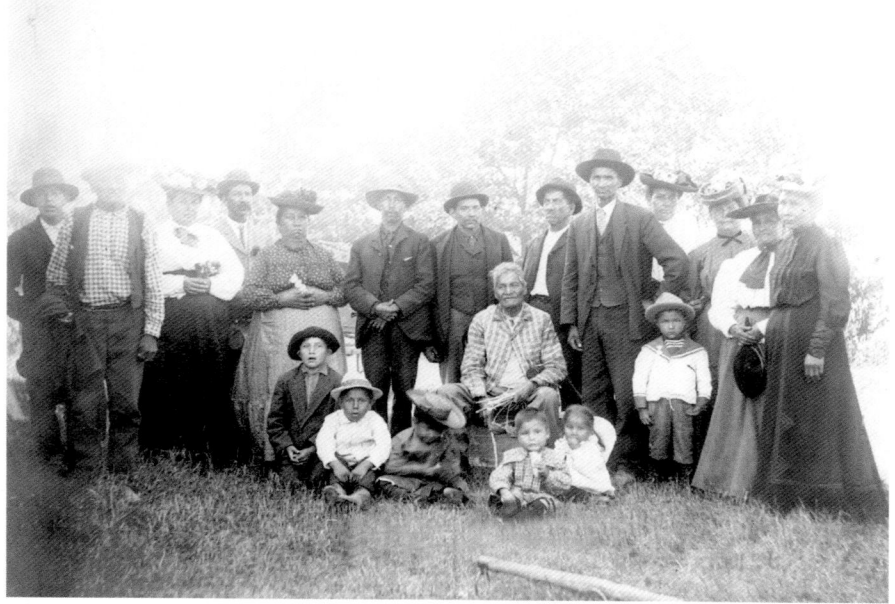

Pottawatomie Indian tribe in the early 1900s wearing "civilized" clothing as Indians tried to assimilate into white society. *Courtesy of the Library of Congress.*

same could be said about the mountain men, the trappers and hunters who had built and abandoned simple huts and cabins before pushing farther west. Log structures chinked with mud and held together by wood pegs now held growing families and stood near what were becoming busy roads. Many of the families who arrived in the area before the 1833 Treaty of Chicago with the Pottawatomie had moved in among the islands of trees in the sea of prairie grass at Elk Grove, Deer Grove, Long Grove, Sarah's Grove and Plum Grove, to name a few.[2] There was a sense of security living among the tall timber that provided shelter and building materials.

Asa Dunton turned over a few shovels full of the rich black prairie soil and decided to stake his claim in the open land that was elevated and well drained. He established his preemption rights to these public lands by declaring his intention of settlement, proving his residence within six months, cultivating the tract within one year and paying the established purchase price of $1.25 an acre. Final title of the homestead was not secured until he had proved his residence thereon for five years.[3]

Asa built a temporary cabin in Deer Grove to shelter his wife and six children: two grown sons, William, then seventeen, and James, age fourteen, and four daughters. Joining them was Asa's sister, Clarissa, who was married

Wagon Ruts Over Pottawatomie Trails

to William Kent, owner of the Old Kent Tavern located between Dundee and Chicago. William Dunton broke ground and planted seed on his land parcel to secure it while his younger brother, James, began building a farm later in 1844. It took a while to register land and have it surveyed and entered into the county plat.

The groves of oaks, pine and hickory fed by nearby creeks provided the necessary wood to build shelters until milled lumber became available. Dunton was fortunate to have two strapping sons to help fell trees producing logs twelve to fifteen feet in length. The wagon horses were hitched to a sled that hauled the logs to the building site. Since he was the first to build a cabin in Deer Grove, Asa did not have the benefit of close neighbors to help with the "house raising." These basic shelters for the family and livestock had to be erected quickly before winter set in and were necessarily crude until amenities such as glass in the windows (replacing sheets of oiled paper) and a wood floor (replacing straw over the dirt) could be put in place. In the fall, before the cold winds came driving in from the northwest, all the logs had to be "re-chinked" where they came together. Rain that would turn to snow continually washed out the porous mud that sealed the log walls.

Until an iron stove could be purchased for their future home and shipped overland by ox teams hauling freight wagons, the fireplace built of sticks and mud or rock and mortar served for both cooking and warming the interior. The fire burned or smoldered continually and plain food was served from iron pots hung from pot hooks sunk into the fire pit wall, skillets resting on roughly forged iron platforms and "Dutch" ovens settled in the glowing faggots and covered with hot coals to form baking ovens for bread and biscuits. Wood buckets filled with hulled corn hominy stood nearby next to hanging wreaths of dried herbs and spices. Vegetables were grown in a small garden and meat was raised on the hoof. A few chickens offered up eggs and food was preserved by salting, smoking, pickling or drying.

With six children to care for, the Duntons had to build a second-floor sleeping loft for the youngsters, which was reached by a ladder, while the main room was partitioned off in the corners for Asa, his wife and the two sons. All of this labor had to be done by hand, and there was always something to be built, repaired, torn down, daubed or sharpened. Formal reading education was catch as catch can for the youngsters, who had enough to do, taking on "women's work" for the daughters and farm chores for the sons. The girls learned how to cook, sew and spin raw fiber into thread and homespun fabric on the "big wheel" that was a standard furnishing in every cabin. All clothes had to be made until much later when ready-made shirts, dresses and denim pants arrived at the trading posts and then dry goods stores.

Arlington Heights, Illinois

They learned about sex and babies by dealing with the farm animals and traveling to nearby groves with their mother to help as assisting midwives for newborns. The boys learned carpentry, metal smithing, rope making and the rigorous demands of animal husbandry.

There would not be a school in the area until 1849, a sixteen- by sixteen-foot structure located at today's northwest corner of Miner and Evergreen Streets. Ten students were taught by Miss Sarah Thornton, who sat at a desk flanked on three sides by benches affixed to the walls. A stove stood in one corner. This school served the farming community that had grown around it for several years before being replaced by a two-room schoolhouse.[4] Teachers were paid by the village and lived with a family since it was considered improper for a single lady to live alone unchaperoned. Books often came from the students' homes, or, if there was money on hand, the McGuffey Readers and spellers were passed out. These long-lived editions were a mainstay of local education up to the turn of the century and beyond. Many of the older residents of the county were familiar with the old McGuffey Readers as well as the McGuffey's spelling book in their youthful days and no doubt a majority of those who used them look back with fond recollection to those days. Those books were read in some sections of the country in the 1830s and were common classroom teaching aids for almost half a century.

Eighth Grade Final Exam—1895

An eighth-grade education in the nineteenth century amounted to a much greater learning experience than might be assumed by modern educators. Because a high school education was considered the equivalent of a college-level matriculation today, finishing grammar school had to prepare students for life. Below are samples of final exam questions from a Midwestern grammar school in 1895. The entire exam of forty-five questions took five hours to complete.

Arithmetic (Time: one hour and fifteen minutes)

1. Name and define the fundamental rules of arithmetic
2. A wagon box is 2 feet deep, 10 feet long and 3 feet wide. How many bushels of wheat will it hold?
3. A load of wheat weighs 3,942 pounds, what is it worth at 50cts/bushel, deducting 1,050 pounds for tare?
4. District No. 33 has a valuation of $35,000. What is the necessary levy

to carry on a school seven months at $50 a month and have $104 for incidentals?
5. What is the cost of a square farm at $15 an acre, the distance of one side being 640 rods?
6. Write a bank check, a promissory note and a receipt

Orthography (Time: one hour)

1. What is meant by the following: alphabet, phonetic, orthography, etymology and syllabication?
2. What are the following, and give examples: trigraph, sub vocals, diphthong, cognate, letters and linguals?
3. Write 10 words frequently mispronounced and indicate pronunciation by use of diacritical marks and syllabication.

Geography (Time: one hour)

1. What is climate? On what does climate depend?
2. Describe the mountains of North America
3. Identify and describe the following: Monrovia, Odessa, Denver, Manitoba, Hecia, Yukon, Helena, Juan Fernandez, Aspinwall and Orinoco.
4. Name all the republics of Europe and name the capital of each[5]

The Dunton family had to remain in the rough existence of the Deer Grove farm until 1841. By then, Asa's title to the land was registered. He then moved himself and his family down to Lemont, where he and his sons worked for needed cash in the rock quarries that turned out stone to be shipped north to the growing Chicago community of four thousand. It was 1847 before he returned to his prairie plots, and many believe that the clapboard house still standing at 612 North Arlington Heights Road was built by Asa Dunton for his wife. James Dunton lived with his parents until 1849, when he was married and built a house at 623 North Arlington Heights Road and, later, a splendid home with a tall mansard roof from which, in 1871, residents of the village of Dunton watched the soaring flames of the Chicago Fire.

It was William Dunton who thought beyond immediate shelter, a job and a family as his goals in life. A single family following a single bottom plough could not make a living on 160 acres of ground no matter how rich the soil. William may have been a stiff-backed Yankee sprig, but he also had a sharp mind and a streak of ambition. First, he sized up the community assets that

17

Arlington Heights, Illinois

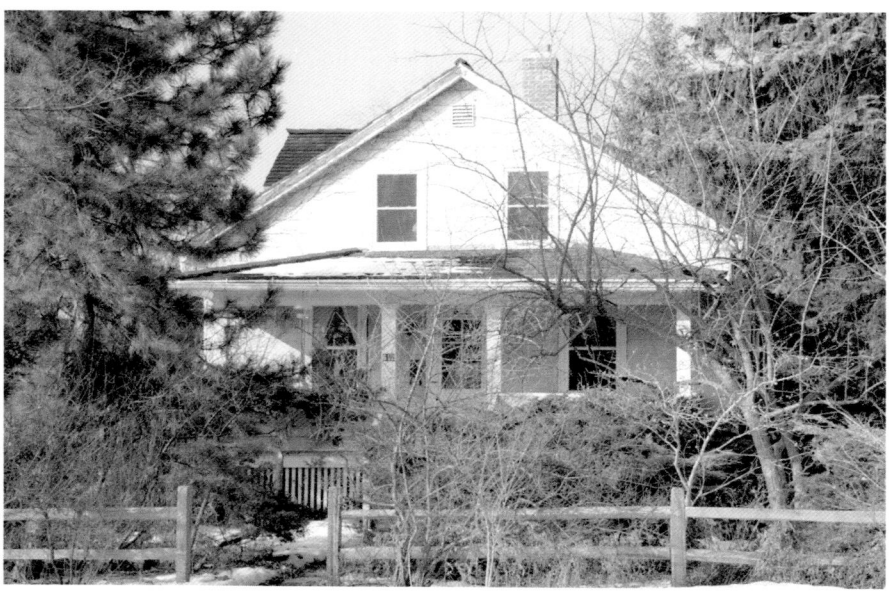

This home, believed to have been built by Asa Dunton, is at 612 North Arlington Heights Road, just north of Euclid. *Photo by Gerry Souter.*

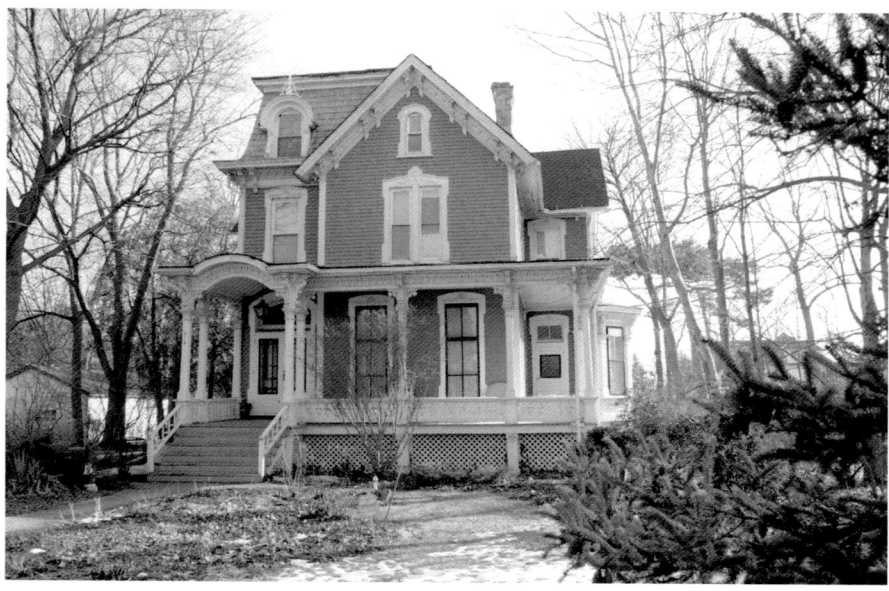

The James Dunton home at 619 North Arlington Heights Road, just north of Euclid. James was the brother of William Dunton. It is believed that he and his family sat on the roof of the home and watched the Chicago Fire. *Photo by Gerry Souter.*

Wagon Ruts Over Pottawatomie Trails

surrounded his plot. A main road that had developed from a Pottawatomie Indian trail would be called State Road and later Arlington Heights Road. It ran past his land from what is now Central Road to Dundee Road. Northeast of Dunton's plot was the diagonal Rand Road or Military Road, so named when the road was widened to accept military wagon trains heading north for the Indian wars. Rand's Tavern was located where the road crossed the Des Plaines River to the southwest. That was a busy thoroughfare, and east of that road was the Milwaukee Trace and a budding town called East Wheeling. It featured a hotel and tavern opened by Joseph Filkins in 1834 and another such establishment under the proprietorship of James Parker that opened its doors in 1840. Taverns were an important part of pioneer life in the prairie wilderness. There were few enough amusements to temper the long hours of work required just to survive. Corn huskings and quilting bees where the women gathered to gossip and sew large quilts of bits and fragments of cloth were community entertainments. The huskings allowed young people to meet and socialize. If in the pile of corn, a young lady or gentleman discovered a red ear, he or she was allowed to kiss any member of the opposite sex who was present. Often musical instruments were brought to the husking and a dance was organized.

But taverns also offered the men a place to belly up, light a black stogy and knock back a cup of Scotch-Irish busthead fresh off the wagon from Ken-tuck-ie. Whiskey was a cheap diversion at twelve and a half cents a quart or forty cents a gallon. Unfortunately, hard work and alcoholism tended to shorten many lives.

The hotels on these busy roads offered travelers aboard the Frink and Walker stagecoach lines a bed for the night, or salesmen for seed and hardware companies a base for their trips to the local farms. In 1837, Russell Wheeler and Charles Daniels established a general store next to Filkin's tavern. When the government designated the Milwaukee Trace to be a post road, a post office for area mail was opened and East Wheeling thrived. In 1838, two hundred people resided in the area.

This success was not lost upon William Dunton. Civilization was coming to this small corner of the prairie and before long Wheeling would become a township. With deliberation and an eye to that future, he subdivided his plot of ground into lots to create what became, on paper, the town of West Wheeling. He then set to work building a balloon-frame clapboard house two stories in height on a corner of his property next to that Indian trail. On December 24, 1845, at a wedding ceremony in Deer Grove, he married Almeda Wood in Asa's one-room log cabin with about twenty friends present. After the ceremony, everyone sat down to a turkey dinner finished off with

Arlington Heights, Illinois

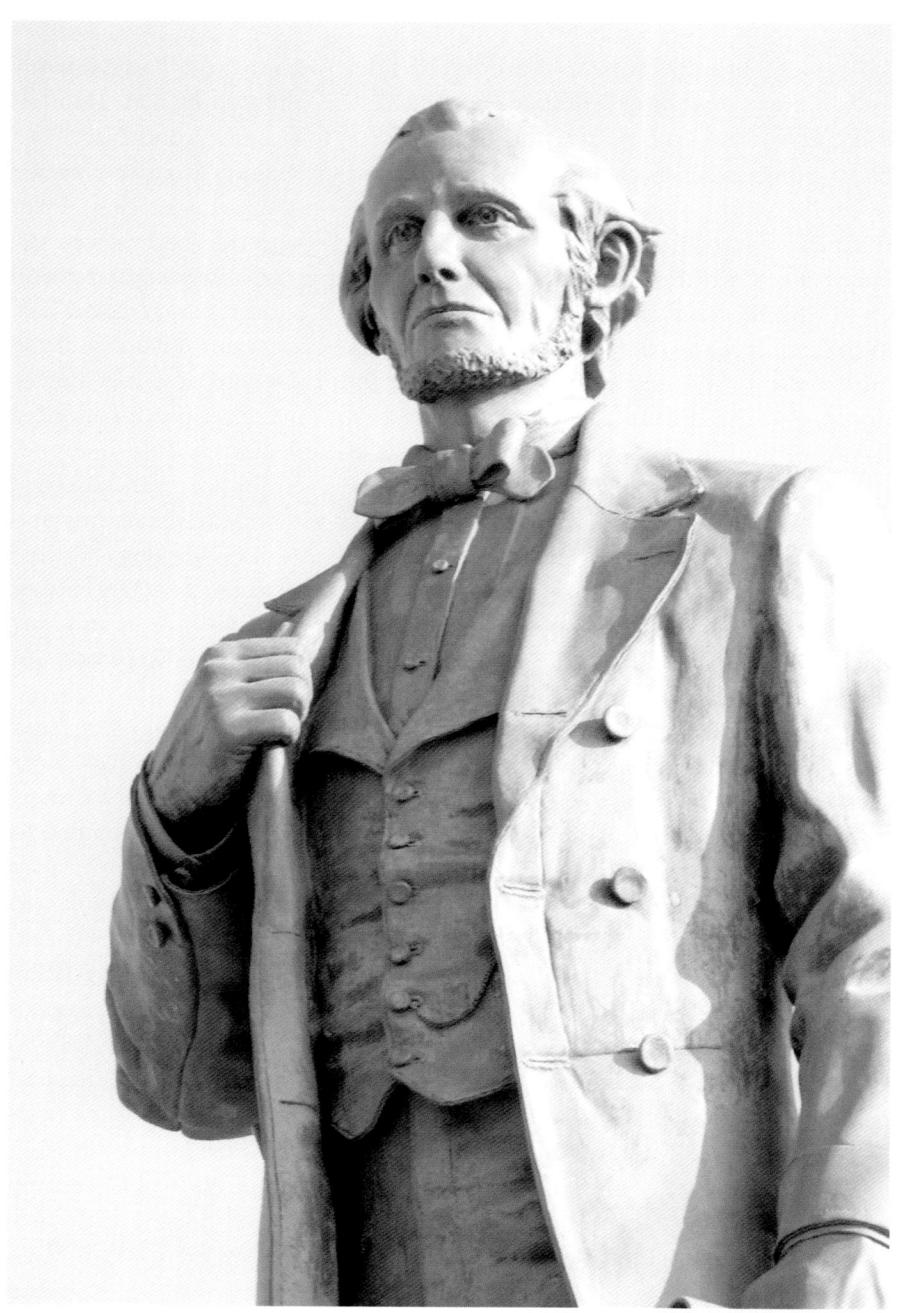

Closeup of William Dunton statue. *Photo by Gerry Souter.*

Wagon Ruts Over Pottawatomie Trails

mince pie. William brought Almeda to their new home, which stood alone on the open prairie. She wrote later, "It was a desolate prairie, no neighbors, no roads, nothing but a little house."

To ease the transition, William decided that they would spend the winter with his folks. To travel to Deer Grove, he cut down two saplings and trimmed them to poles. He bent up the ends and tied them in place with rope to form sled runners. He built a seat for two fashioned from a dry goods box on planks that spanned the two poles. It was called a "jumper" and was drawn by one horse or a team. Jumpers were also made from old skis and barrel staves. There would be time to set up housekeeping in the spring.

The roads were named after the farms and properties they passed when the first plat of Wheeling Township was officially registered on March 23, 1851. The road past William's home became Dunton Road. Taxes were a few cents for each $100 worth of real estate and personal property plus $2 or one day's labor on the roads by each male inhabitant except for paupers, lunatics, idiots and others exempted by law. Dogs were taxed at $1 each and the money went to pay for damages for farm animals killed by dogs. At the end of the year, money left over went into the fund set aside for scraping the roads.[6]

The community scheduled township meetings and East Wheeling, near the junction of the Milwaukee Trace and the Des Plaines River, became the hub of settlement and most activity. In Chicago, however, there were plans afoot to change all that. Railroads had begun to snake their way into the hinterlands from major population centers to serve the surrounding farm communities. They were in competition with canals and canalboats but offered a less expensive solution and greater flexibility when it came to creating their routes. By 1848, the Galena & Chicago Union Railroad had laid track from downtown Chicago west a few miles and had bought a third-hand steam engine, wood tender and some rolling stock to haul wheat and a few adventurous passengers over its strap iron rails. This "Pioneer" locomotive and its train was the first of many rail lines that thrust out from Chicago, which became the railroad hub of the United States.

Another group of investors bought land to create a rail right of way northwest, aimed at Wisconsin. This Wisconsin Land Company laid track in 1848 and soon reached the town of Rand, today known as Des Plaines, named after Socrates Rand, who owned a popular tavern. The idea was to continue the railroad parallel to Rand Road—the old Military Road—up to Cary and from there to Crystal Lake and end up at Janesville, Wisconsin. The company would continue buying property along the route where trading posts had sprung up. Around these posts they envisioned towns would grow and

Arlington Heights, Illinois

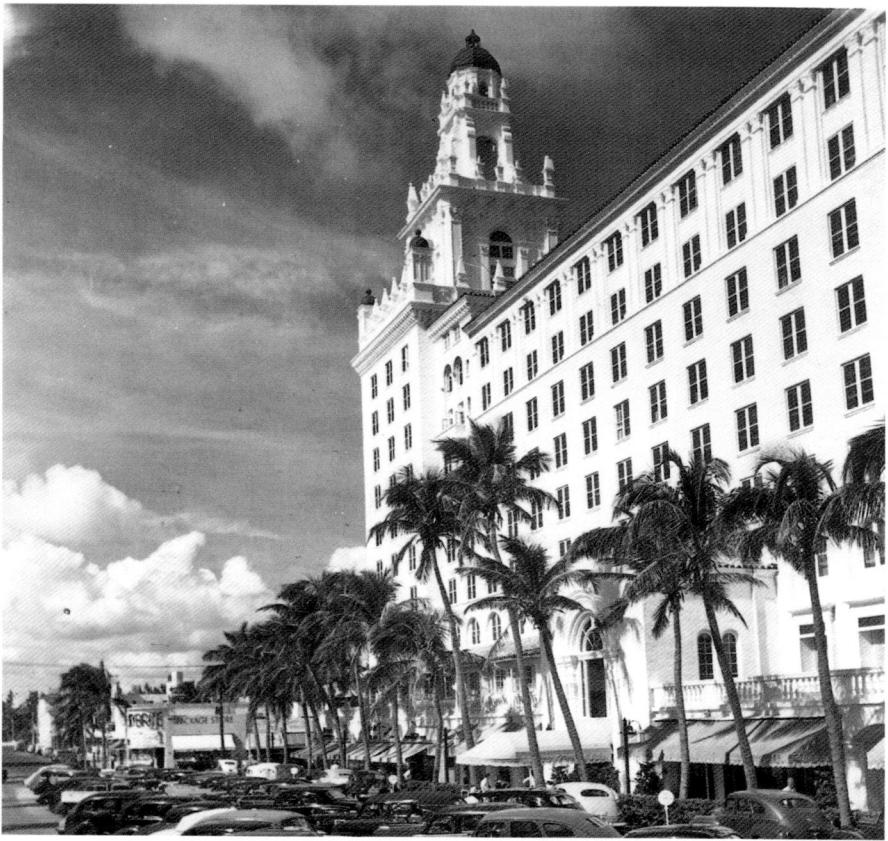

Early map of the Arlington Heights area. *Courtesy of the Arlington Heights Historical Society.*

everyone would make sacks of money from transporting goods, farm produce and people to and from Chicago clear to the northern forests and farms of Wisconsin. It was a bold business plan and was not lost upon William Dunton, who had a ready-made town site plotted out. He had become a well-known figure in the area and served as moderator of the town meetings in 1850.

Dunton presented himself to the Wisconsin Land Company with an idea and a deal. Using what must have been considerable powers of persuasion, he convinced the Illinois & Wisconsin Railroad to shift its tracks west through his little community of West Wheeling and then on up through Deer Grove to Crystal Lake. To lubricate the venture, he put up sixteen acres of land cleared for the right of way for $350. The deed was signed on August 18, 1853, and recorded on March 24, 1854. The town's name on Section 29 was penned in as Dunton.

Wagon Ruts Over Pottawatomie Trails

With that bit of business done and the success of his real estate venture secured, William and Almeda journeyed up to Deer Grove to spend the winter with his father, Asa, in the old farmstead. When spring arrived, William found the surveying crew for the I&WRR had been through his town site, and the tracks were scheduled to pass right through the living room of his new two-story house. There was nothing for it but to jack up the house and move it to the northeast side of Dunton Road, which would later be called State Road. In 1854, a passenger and freight depot was built alongside the single track between today's Dunton and Evergreen Avenues. The first sign on it read "Elk Grove" after the nearest post office and then "West Wheeling" and, finally, "Dunton," which became official.

Asa and James moved into homes in the town and, bit by bit, stores replaced trading posts and cattle pens were erected near trackside. A platform was built for the daily milk train from the north to pick up and drop off milk cans, and in 1860, the Union Hotel, saloon and livery stable were doing good business on Campbell Street. The town of Dunton, astride the railroad track, was a going concern and never looked back.

As the railroads were extending the transportation web that began on the East Coast, adding tracks to the growing road, canal and river traffic network, in Europe, social changes were taking place that would add to the United States' melting pot. Between 1816 and 1848, there was a major population surge that had devastating effects in France and Germany. The middle classes—bourgeoisie—swelled and liberal factions demanded parliamentary governments. Constitutional republics replaced the autocratic rule of kings and ducal states. In Germany, passions ran deep as the largest part of the population sought representation. While the politicians and activists clamored, Germany also faced crop harvest failures in 1846. With the population growing from 24,800,000 in 1816 to 34,400,000 in 1848, there was less food to feed them. Besides food for the belly, food for the soul was also diminishing. Writers, artisans and musicians found the opportunity for creativity choked off by the internal conflict.

The only choice for those caught between the liberals and the divine right autocrats was to flee the country. In 1846, 95,000 Germans left; in 1847, 110,000. The Revolution of 1848, which aroused so many hopes, reduced the number of emigrants: it fluctuated between 80,000 and 90,000 from 1848 to 1850. Then, in 1851, there were 113,000 emigrants; in 1852, 162,000; in 1853, 163,000; and in 1854, the number reached 300,000.[7]

A great portion of this major tide of emigration washed up on the shores of the United States. These immigrants arrived in a continuing

Arlington Heights, Illinois

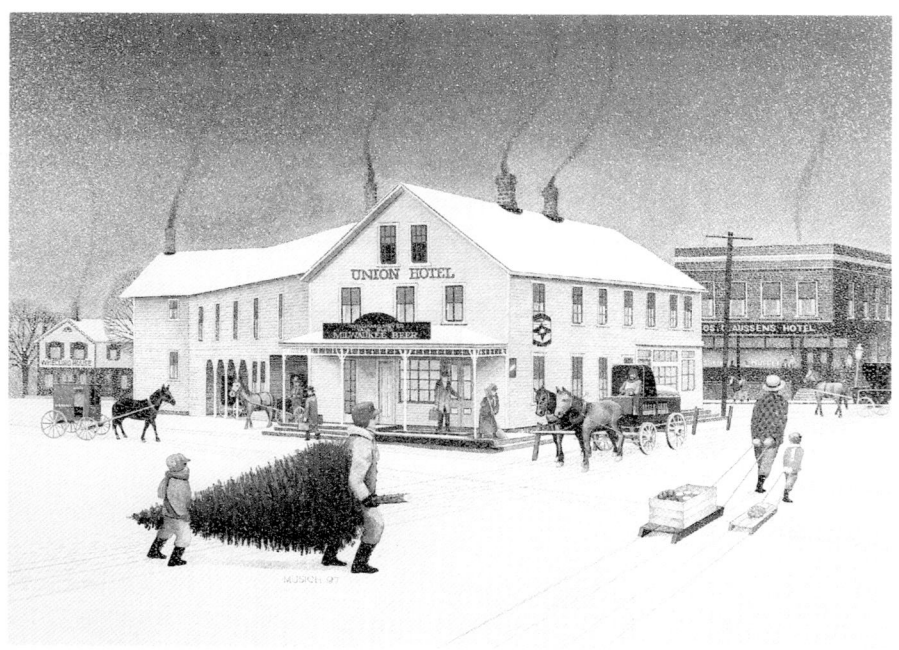

Painting of the Union Hotel in the winter. The Union, on the corner of what is now the Chase Bank, was one of the first buildings in what was then the town of Dunton. *Painting by Jack Musich.*

flood as the eastern United States was undergoing its own population growth problems. The original Yankees and Scotch-Irish had swelled their numbers, flooded down into the South and Southwest and crossed the Appalachian Mountains into the rich bottomlands and Mississippi watershed. Their wagons carried them north to the Minnesota forests and to the beginning of the Great Central Plain, the vast savannah that would be submerged beneath the plow and become the nation's breadbasket. Following these trails westward came the uprooted Germans, stunned by the richness of the land and its immensity.

These transplanted Germans were not ragged refugees but were literate and brought their culture, means and businesses with them in their wagons and on their backs. They had the funds, and land developers in Chicago did a booming business. Family after family came down Rand Road or stepped off the old steam train at the new Dunton depot and asked in halting English where they could locate their piece of the dream. The "Dutchies" had arrived.

Chapter 2

GROWING UP BY THE TRACKS

During those early years in Dunton when the paint of the depot was still fresh and the land plots mostly existed on William Dunton's 1854 map, the town site was more an idea than a reality. The 1840s and '50s brought more farmers than shopkeepers, hoteliers or blacksmiths. The railroad was still a flag stop—trains stopping only for a red ball hung from a pole next to the track or a red lantern at night—except for mail when a post office opened at the rear of the Union Hotel. Even then, the train barely slowed down to drop the mail sack and pick up the outgoing post in a leather bag that hung from a swinging arm at trackside. But the growing number of farmsteads quickly produced a demand for services that drew the necessary entrepreneurs.

The farmers, as had been the pioneer homesteaders who preceded them, were accustomed to doing for themselves or doing without. The influx of Germans came with their sleeves rolled up and added their skills to the mix. In 1844, Michael W. Winkels was typical of the new arrivals to the area. He was thirty-eight years old and had traveled by rail from New York to Chicago with his wife and one son and then headed by wagon out into the country thirty "English miles," where he put down his roots. Michael wrote his relatives in Prussia (translated from the original German):

> *I bought me a farm of 160 acres which, according to German measure makes 200 morhen, at $2.50 an acre, or six marks in German money. The land lies in a good situation and also a beautiful neighborhood. Also we have a very fine meadow land upon which the grass is so high, it reaches above my head. This will perhaps seem unbelievable to you, but it is true. I would not have believed it myself had I not seen it. The forest is composed of many trees and hazel bushes like none as are found in Germany and they*

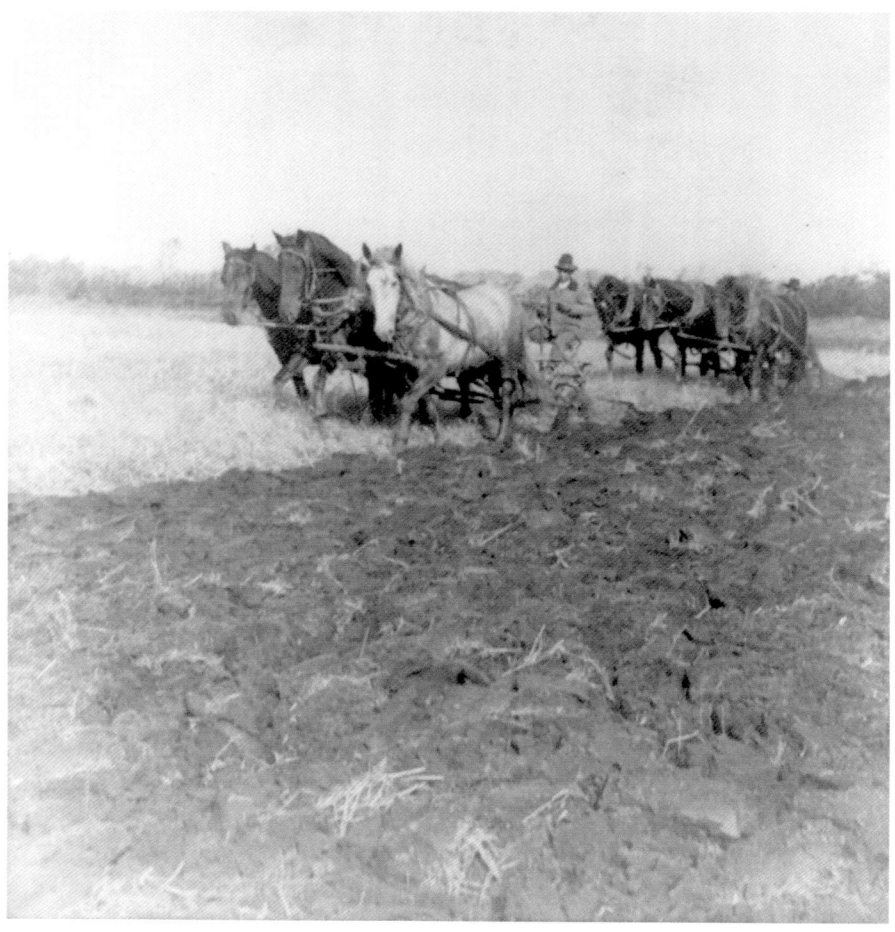

Plowing the fields in the late nineteenth century. *Courtesy of the Library of Congress.*

grow in abundance. Also in the woods, the wild lemons (plums) grow in abundance. When we bought the land we hardly knew what to say as we glimpsed the splendid fruit and the high grass. We also bought two oxen that are as heavy as the largest one finds in Germany. Also a double span wagon and cooking machine (cook stove) which is very artfully constructed. One can cook upon four fires at once and at the same time have an oven for baking. We also bought two cows and a plow besides household gear that one needs on the farm. The oxen cost $40 and the wagon $33. The cook stove cost $22 with utensils included and the plow, $7 and the two cows, $24.00.

When we once get things somewhat arranged we can keep one hundred head of stock on our place. Here it is not like in Germany that one must

Growing Up by the Tracks

support the cattle with his labor: here, cattle support themselves. They run out day and night—cows, hogs, oxen, horses and so on. Cows come home evenings and mornings by themselves. Feed is absolutely free. One can make hay where he wishes and as much as he wants without paying for it. Here, one knows nothing about taxes. One does not need to worry about beggars as they do in Germany. Here, a man works for himself. Here, one is equal to another. We no longer long for Germany. Every day we thank the Dear Lord that he has brought us, so to speak, out of slavery and into paradise.

Costuming in America is similar to that of the best people in Germany. It is particularly handsome in the case of men. One cannot distinguish the farmer from the gentleman—they all stand on the same planes. If a woman should cross the street without a hat, she would be laughed at.[8]

With new arrivals like the Winkels family in the northwest prairie, a casual visitor to Dunton in the 1840s and '50s heard German spoken on the dirt streets and plank sidewalks as readily as English. Each day the growing cluster of clapboard stores with false fronts that clustered close to the railroad track was wafted with coal smoke as a steam locomotive hauling a variety of freight and passenger cars clattered and chugged into town, its bell clanging. Horses tethered near the depot tugged at their reins, whinnied and snorted. Vented steam hissed from the churning pistons and the heat from the firebox made those waiting at trackside turn away. Each arrival was an event.

The original railroad, modeled on the Galena & Chicago Union Railroad, used flat strap iron rails nailed to wood ties. With wear, the strap iron sprung loose and coiled up like a snake, ripping through the underbellies of the cars and killing people and livestock. In 1855, the shape steel rail used today replaced the iron strap and the five-foot separation between rails was compressed into the new Standard Gauge: four feet, eight inches.

By 1857, the Illinois and Wisconsin had merged with the Rock Island Railroad, which became the Chicago, St. Paul & Fond du lac Railroad Company (CSP&FL). Both freight and passenger trains were running, but the passenger trains had to turn off the single-track main line onto a siding at Rand to let freights rumble past. Commodities and goods paid for the service offered to passengers. Dunton was a farm town and shipping a four-bottom plow was worth more than a seat in one of the wood coaches. Commuting to Chicago had not yet become common. What jobs there were in the town site served the local population: dry goods, blacksmithing, wagon building, crop milling and the medical arts. Of course there were the saloons, such as the Union and Wheeling House, as well as restaurants that offered simple fare with quick turnover due to short-lived storage and preservation methods. Hotel rooms were available to transients, mostly sales representatives, "drummers" who represented large hardware, durable goods and farm implement companies in Chicago and back East.

Until a second track was laid along the right of way, train arrivals produced a flurry of activity since schedules were critical to free the blocked track and keep rail traffic running. Though the web of railroads was creeping across the country, schedules were all based on local time, and where time zones met, adjustments had to be made. These discrepancies caused many head-on collisions and deaths as trains traveling in opposite directions ended up on the same track. Standard Time consistent across the country was not instituted until the railroads did so on November 18, 1883. Even then, some communities were slow to accept it. The city of Detroit kept its own local time until 1900.

The 1857 passenger schedule had two trains running daily in each direction. The southbound train arrived at Dunton at 12:52 p.m. and pulled into Chicago at 1:55 p.m. The other southbound train stopped at the Dunton depot at 8:52 p.m. and arrived in Chicago at 10:00 p.m. Coming back from the big city to Dunton required catching the 7:00 a.m. and arriving at 9:00 a.m., or catching the afternoon passenger express at 2:05 p.m. and arriving at Dunton at 3:05 p.m. These were hardly commuter specials, but compared to horse-drawn transport over the same distance, their speed seemed miraculous, sometimes touching thirty-five miles an hour. A trip into Chicago was a major adventure since most people living in rural communities rarely journeyed more than twenty-five miles from home during their lifetime.[9]

Dunton's original boundaries cover about eighty acres drawn on a rectangular grid, with Euclid Street as its northernmost boundary and the tracks running down the center cutting across State Road (formerly Dunton's Road), Campbell Street, Evergreen, Dunton Avenue and Vail Avenue. Its streets coated the hems of long dresses and tall boots with a mixture of churned mud and animal manure. Every shop had a cast-iron boot scraper outside the door. Out in back of every establishment was a minimum of one two-holer outhouse. In the winter, the wind that whipped snow between the houses and shops carried with it the smell of burning wood and coal. Ashes scooped from hand-carried scuttles were mixed with the snow and ice to prevent falls and twisted ankles. A two-span wagon clinked and rumbled over the snow-choked avenues towing a board scraper that angled the powder into drifts that could be shoveled down. Town kids and farm kids, who had come in with their parents to stock up on supplies and hear the latest news, used the piled snow as makeshift sledding hills.

Growing Up by the Tracks

From every shop and saloon window came the orange glow of kerosene lamps or, at Christmastime, the flicker of candles decorating the trees hung with handmade ornaments. In the summer, everything was flung open to the cooling breezes, and old men and farmers who had completed their commerce sat on the depot benches between trains or gathered on the porch beneath the overhang of the Union Hotel. A bowl of pickled eggs might be passed around—certain to be covered with cheesecloth against the swarms of bluebottle flies that rose up with the heat from the layer of animal waste that gathered everywhere and was particularly dense at the large manure pile just off the edge of downtown. Horse stables, cow paths, hog wallows and chicken pens produced enough secondhand feed to thoroughly ammoniate the atmosphere. What the flies left behind was picked clean by the mosquitoes. Ponds and sluggish creeks produced clouds of the pests, and people grew accustomed to the scent of oil of citronella liberally applied to exposed skin. The ponds and creeks also signified a high water table, so wells were dug to a relatively shallow depth before striking water. In town, cast-iron hand pumps brought up what was needed and stored it in cisterns along with rain water. On the farm, a tipping beam with a bucket at one end and counterbalanced with a weight on the other was used to dunk into a shallow well, raise the bucket and swing the beam to one side.

In the town, certain rhythms evolved over the years. Most people found themselves a "third place" to be. Their first place was home, the second was work and the third was special, a place where they met with friends to commune, enjoy a pipe, bring out the knitting or just sit in companionable silence. Some places were like magnets, welcoming and comfortable. Farmers stopped in at Redeker's store and gravitated to his adjoining house, where his wife produced fresh-baked coffee cake and a cup that stirred the soul.

Herman Redeker came to the village from Germany with his grandparents and father in 1882 at age eleven, and his family erected a brick store at the northeast corner of Vail and Davis Streets. His grandfather built the business by always adding something "extra" to each order. The old man trained Herman's mother in serving customers.

"Always give extra measure. Weigh out the pound of sugar they ask for, then give them an extra scoop. Cookies the same, add a few extra. And an extra half yard for the housewife buying material for her daughter's Sunday dress."[10]

Another "third place" was the Page Blacksmith Shop at 13 West Davis Street where the smithy's forge rang and the sparks flew as men sat outside in the shade, amid the pungent aroma of cigar smoke mixed with the stink of seared iron and flaring charcoal. There was always something heavy that needed to be shifted and that led to contests to see who could lift the most.

Arlington Heights, Illinois

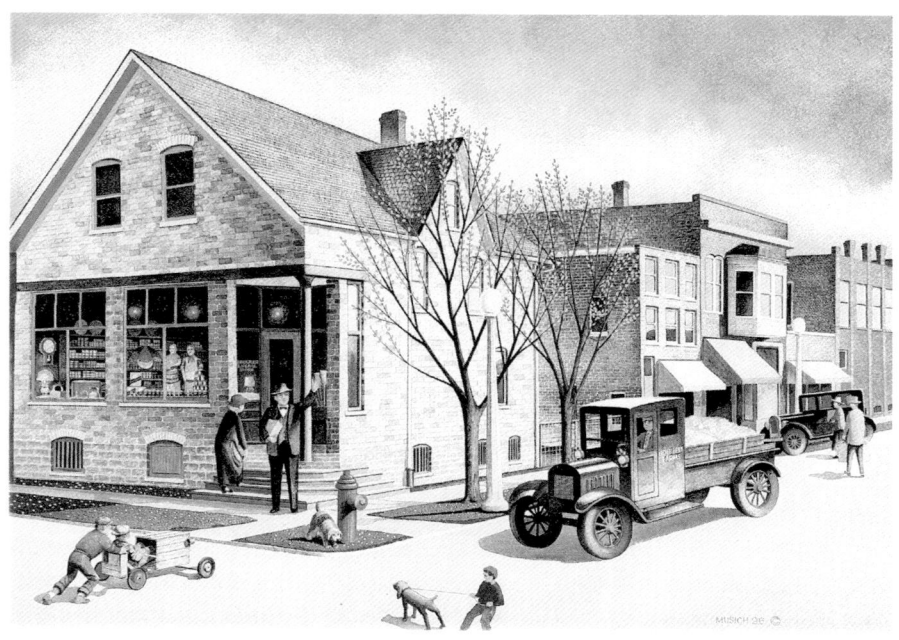

Redeker's general store, northeast corner of Vail Avenue and Campbell Street, late 1800s. The building is now the site of Harry's, a restaurant and sports bar. *Painting by Jack Musich.*

    Those rhythms of daily town life often opened with bawling and mooing. The morning ritual began early with the lead cow's bell clunking with each desultory bovine stride down Campbell Street. A boy with a switch stayed near the two-cow parade as they passed haystacks and orchards. Overhead, meadowlarks swooped in clusters. Underfoot, pheasants dodged into the fields or broke cover in a rush of flapping wings and their twittering cry. A meadow stretched where Ridge Avenue runs today, and there the cows munched contentedly until fetched in the evening.

    Cattle were a big part of the commerce that flourished in downtown Dunton. Between where Vail and Highland Avenues crossed the track, cattle pens were constructed on the south side. Farmers selected the cows for transport into the Chicago Stock Yards, herded them over the roads and drove them in a day early. Each pen held a salt lick, and during the night, the cattle licked that salt block, but there was no water in the pens. People living in homes near the pens were entertained all night by the bawling of the thirsty cows. Come morning, the cows were watered and they drank deeply before the empty cattle cars arrived, adding water to their weight to bring a higher price at the scales.

Growing Up by the Tracks

Dairy cows also thrived on the rich hay made from prairie grass, and the gallons of fresh milk they produced had a ready market in Chicago. Before dawn, when the southbound milk train was due, the farmers brought in their full milk cans to a platform that had been erected at trackside. Once the loaded milk train chugged and clanked away just after 4:00 a.m., the farmers adjourned to the Wheeling House, which had opened in 1855 at Evergreen Avenue and Campbell Street, where the Lauterburgs prepared a buffet of baked beans, soup, stew and fresh bread for the hungry men.

Livestock was part of everyday life during those early days growing up by the railroad track. Fresh meat was available only from cattle, hogs, chickens and ducks penned up behind most homes. Slaughtered livestock hung in sheds over cordwood fires and was smoked or dried and "jerked" into strips. Small cuts of pork and fowl were packed in crocks surrounded by a thick glaze of their own rendered fat. Later, the wife brought the crock up from the cool basement or root cellar, opened it, scraped off the fat and created a confit of the kind that chefs back east served up for top dollar. Connoisseurs in New York restaurants prized the salty, robust "country" flavor. Hard work and survival in Dunton, Illinois, burned off those cholesterol-packed calories while city dandies just grew fat.

Vegetables and fruits from the growing number of orchards were eaten fresh and the surplus was "canned," "put up" or "laid by," depending on where you came from. Pickling and salting were preservations that continued even after the work of Louis Pasteur demonstrated how heat and boiling killed bacteria that caused spoilage.

One sure sign of growth were the community projects that went forward. Besides the depot, milk can–loading platform and cattle pens that were built, storage silos for sugar beets and coal were raised. Grain elevators accommodated corn and wheat for shipping and for sale. Near State Road on the north side of the tracks, the first mill was built so grains could be sold as flour by the sack. Farmers who made the long ride into town to shop or bring products for sale could water their horses at a cast-iron fountain kept filled by a float pump. The service cost a two-dollar subscription fee that went into the town fund.

Of all the community projects that came from the farms and homes of Dunton, Illinois, in the year 1860, none was as important as recruiting sons, husbands and fathers for the Union army. The rattle of drums sounded in the towns along the railroad track as recruiters set up their tables and stacks of enlistment forms. Nearly every vertical surface was nailed with a poster offering cash to able-bodied men who would fight to preserve the Union and punish the "secesh" (secessionist) Rebels. Illinois regiments filled up fast and no true patriot wanted to miss out on such an adventure.

Arlington Heights, Illinois

Big, strapping German farm boys stood in line along with Yankee clerks to sign their names or make their marks on the roster. Quotas were based on population and Dunton easily answered the call. Military trains were already heading north up toward Minnesota where the Sioux Indians had chosen this time to begin slaughtering settlers and burning farms in retaliation for a number of injustices. So each day locomotives rolled through town, some laden with soldiers going north while others collected recruits with their suitcases and sack lunches on their way south to Chicago to join their regiment. Old men who had fought in the Blackhawk Indian war sat on the steps of the Union Hotel puffing their pipes and watched as a generation of young men waved goodbye to their sweethearts and husbands kissed their children before boarding. Flags waved. A German band tried to play "Nearer My God to Thee" with some verve and military cadence. The only other martial tune they knew was "Dixie."[11]

One young man who stepped aboard the recruiting train was twenty-two-year-old Charles Sigwalt. The ink was barely dry on his naturalization papers when he signed up with Company I of the Eighth Regiment, Illinois Volunteer Infantry, First Brigade, Second Division of the Fourth Army Corps, Army of the Cumberland. Throughout the war he kept a diary in beautiful copperpoint handwriting, finding time to lean back against a wagon wheel, a tree stump or the edge of a ditch to record daily events in his small book.

During the battle for Atlanta, General George Thomas, "the Rock of Chickamauga," was bringing his command into the fight. On July 20, 1864, they paused for a break in the march at the edge of a broad field near Peach Tree Creek. Charles Sigwalt was one of many men who felt exposed with that field on their flank and began tearing down a fence to form some cover. He wrote:

> *We went a little way to the rear. We had no orders to tear down this* [split rail] *fence, but like lightning we tore at the rails until we had stakes in the ground and stacked the wood rails until they was musket-proof.*
>
> *No sooner had they started when John B. Hood and regiments of rebel troops came boiling out of the woods on the far side of that field.*
>
> *We heard this tremendous yell. Someone shouted, "The Rebels are coming!" We grabbed our muskets and fell in. The 15th Missouri was coming over our works and the Rebels was right behind them.*
>
> *They came at a long trot, shoulder to shoulder; some dressed in butternut and gray, others in ragged farm clothes, some in boots, others barefoot. They came with a rush and a blood curdling yell. Bayonet points caught the sun that quickly faded behind clouds of black powder gun smoke.*

Growing Up by the Tracks

"Here they come! Come on, boys, get ready! I see the flags. A shout from our line: 'Give 'em hell!'"

A muttering volley snapped out from behind the fence rails.

Now they were within 25 yards of our breastworks and we banged away with our muskets straight into them.

As quickly as it started, the charge piled up on the bodies of the dead and dying. The thicket of bayonets thinned as muskets fell into the field grass. Screams of attack were replaced by screams of agony. Someone down the Yankee line shouted,

"My God, but we've repulsed them!" And the Union infantry began counter attacking. A riderless horse galloped by.

They made seven separate charges on our brigade. We repulsed them every time. After a while, they returned to their breastworks and it was over.

His face still blackened by gunpowder, he spit out paper cartridge remnants and drank deep from his canteen. In the heavy-breathing quiet after the battle punctuated by the groans of the wounded and shouts of the sergeants, Sigwalt wrote, "Had we not erected that barricade, they would have whipped us and moved our army back across Peach Tree Creek where we would have been shot or drowned. Soon, we will be marching on Atlanta and see what that place has for us."[12]

He finished that diary later and sent it dutifully home to Dunton to his older brother, Mathias, as he had sent many letters about his life under arms. He saw action in sixteen major battles, and his younger brother Jacob was killed in the Battle of Stone's River. The boy's body was never found. At the end of the war, Sigwalt mustered out and went back to the town by the railroad track. Later, he became village clerk, postmaster and, still later, village president. Charles Sigwalt was quite elderly when one day he was delivering some flowers and never saw the locomotive that hit him. Even then, he lingered for four years and died in 1930 at age ninety-six. Virtually the entire town of Dunton turned out to see him home. The colors of his regiment and the flag he had defended flew in the procession while three drummers and three buglers kept the cadence.

During the war years, the price of Dunton beef went up, as did its dairy products and produce. The hard work of running the farms, managing the shops, tending to livestock and keeping the youngsters in school fell to the women and those men too old to fight. With the railroad came the telegraph and Chicago newspapers and with those came the casualty reports. Young Warren Kennicott, the son of Joseph and Marie Kennicott, was cut down during the bloody battles at Gettysburg, Pennsylvania. In all, of the sixty men who left to fight, seventeen Dunton men did not return to their prairie home.

Though Illinois was deep in Yankee territory, not everyone supported the Union cause. To smoke out any Southern sympathizers, a local "vigilance committee" was formed. One night, a closet Rebel cut down the town flagpole. The committee wired the governor for suggestions on how to deal with this threat. The governor, the Honorable Richard Yates, penned, "Shoot the man on sight and I will pardon the man who does the shooting."[13]

With the conclusion of the Civil War in 1865, the Industrial Revolution came boiling into town, with manufacturing rising up to replace the original farm services economy. Over the next thirty years, the sleepy agrarian community became transformed. Just before the war, the railroad changed hands yet again and was purchased by the Chicago & Northwestern Railway Company for the sum of $10,849,938. Both freight and passenger traffic over the line increased considerably. With improved rail service, a population surge occurred after the war, with a particularly large influx of Germans during the 1870s. The town site grew to 250 acres and more than 1,200 people lived in the village proper.

The Great Chicago Fire of 1871 lit up the sky to the south, and many villagers watched the flames ravage the city from the rooftop of James Dunton's new home on State Road. Rebuilding that city drew many skilled workers from the outlying communities: carpenters, stonemasons and pipe fitters, and the clay deposits in nearby Northbrook were worked overtime to produce bricks. Likewise, a labor pool unemployed by the fire looked elsewhere for jobs.

The downtown area saw a number of changes, including adding two more boardinghouses to compete with the expanding Union Hotel. A tailor shop and a buggy rental opened their doors, as did another blacksmith and a furniture factory that also doubled as a funeral parlor. John Bray and Benjamin Kinder operated a hardware store at 8 North Dunton Avenue from 1869 to 1872, when it and James Dunton's store burned down in a fire. Shortly thereafter, flatcars rolled into town on the C&NW to unload a few tons of brick, and the shops that went up became known as the "Brick Block"; they are still part of Dunton Avenue.

Across the tracks, a business became an Arlington Heights fixture. F.W. "Pop" Muller came to the village in 1872 along with the second phase of German immigration that was fleeing enforced military recruitment for what became the Franco-Prussian War. These new immigrants settled into property that had formerly been owned by the original New England

Growing Up by the Tracks

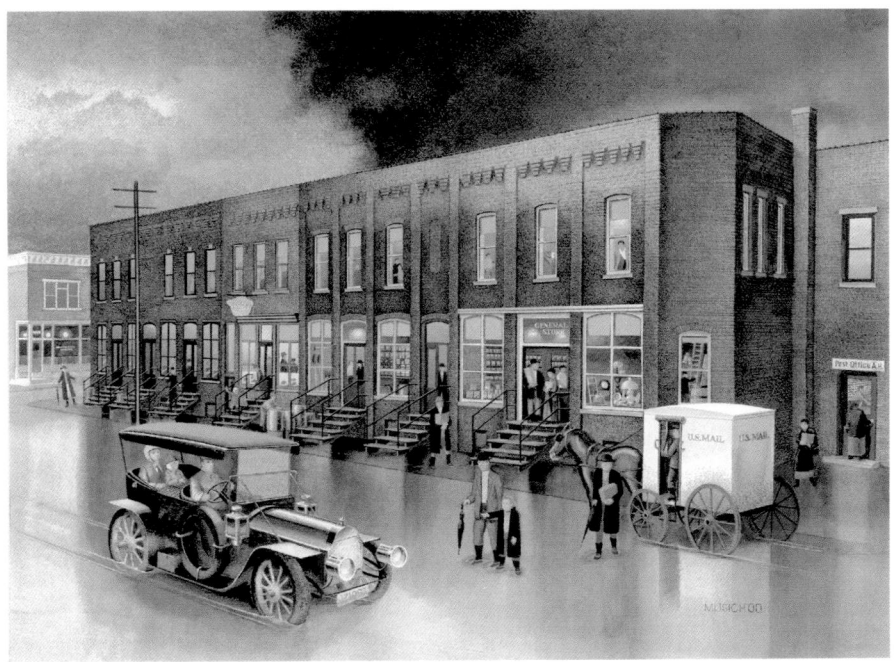

Dunton Avenue, 1900s. This was known as the "Brick Block." *Painting by Jack Musich.*

Yankee settlers. Muller bought a house on South Dunton Avenue and began bottling soft drinks, including ginger ale, strawberry soda, lemon soda and sarsaparilla, in the barn behind his house. From nine o'clock in the morning to nine o'clock at night, the work continued and the business grew. He built a two-story house on property at the corner of Vail Avenue and Fremont Street and moved the business into the "English basement." He began delivering his carbonated beverages with a horse and wagon, and as his product moved into new markets as far away as Diamond Lake and Itasca, he bought a gas-powered truck. Eventually, a two-story brick building was built farther down Fremont Street, with living quarters above the manufacturing and bottling works.

A regular real estate boom was transforming the prairie northwest of Chicago by the mid-1870s, and developers were quick to buy up lots for housing and commercial development. One wily promoter, Mr. R.B. Mitchell, was particularly successful. As the village grew, locals began to feel the name "Dunton" did not have a prosperous ring to it. So far, the village had been called "Elk Grove" after the nearest post office and then "Bradley" after a friend of William Dunton, but this was foiled because of another "Bradley" in Illinois. Then the name "Arlington" was suggested (some believe Mitchell was responsible). There was already another "Arlington" in Illinois, but since the village was located on a high point in the northwest topography, the name "Heights" was appended. Everyone wanted to live on a height.

R.B. Mitchell promptly published a promotional newsletter in 1875, the *Arlington Heights Gazette and Real Estate Bulletin*. In it he preached the gospel of rural living to Chicagoans struggling with crowded city life: "Go to Arlington Heights. You can secure a home of your own in a few years, merely by the rents you are paying now to the greedy landlord."

The Bray family ran their hardware store until 1881, when it was sold to John Burkitt, who added jewelry to the hardware line. Later, Richard Bray and his close friend and partner, Anthony Kates, bought back the store and, in response to the growing dairy production in the area, began assembling milk cans in the rear of the building. This new business flourished and they scoured the countryside for tinsmiths to create an inventory of cans to stock a new three-story frame building at 11 West Davis Street. Expanding further, they finally erected a three-story brick factory housing Bray & Kates Mfrs of Milk Cans in 1897. By 1900, another flood of Eastern European immigrants arrived, primarily from Czechoslovakia, and went straight to work for Bray & Kates after high school, causing the factory to be called the "Arlington University."

This immigration surge created another cultural phenomenon that was discovered by Arlington Heights historian Margery Frisbie. As she tells it, around the turn of the century, the Eastern Europeans took up residence on the south side of the village and also found work at the Creamery Package Company for ten cents an hour. This wage did not permit many luxuries, or even the wherewithal to afford a proper funeral when one of their numbers breathed his last.

Fortunately, there was—and always has been—a number of funeral parlors in the village, and one of them offered to bury the industrious, but impoverished, deceased for free. Having pride in their craft, the parlor staff laid out the body with as much care as with their more prosperous clients. Curiously, when the coffins were returned from the wakes, which were held in the family homes, the body was often crumpled down in the bottom of the pine box like a heap of old clothes. The funeral director discovered that it was still the custom for the grieving family to prop the coffin upright so friends and family could be photographed one last time with the deceased and the photos could be sent to distant relatives. To the director's relief, that custom faded away in time.

The Arlington Heights funeral industry endured one other cultural divide, as described to Margery by Myrtle Lauterburg, sister to one of the longest

Growing Up by the Tracks

established funeral parlor owners in the village. Through the early years and up to the not-too-distant past, there was a religious hostility between the Lutherans ("Dutchies) and the Catholics ("Cat-licks"). This antagonism dated back to the day Martin Luther nailed his ninety-five complaining theses to the Wittenburg cathedral door in 1517. In this Illinois farm town, however, religion dictated who buried the parishioners' earthly remains. There were Catholic funeral parlors and Lutheran funeral parlors.

In 1920, Uriel Reese was looking to sell his undertaking business at Campbell and Evergreen, but he only wanted to sell to another Catholic. According to Myrtle, he had cornered the Catholic burial business by using his horse teams to drive the priests around the village on their pastoral calls. He managed to rope in most of the Methodists as well. Walter Oehler of Des Plaines wanted to buy it, but Oehler was a Lutheran; he approached A.J. Lauterburg, who was Catholic, to go into partnership and purchase Reese's business. Reese sold it to both because he wanted to be sure a Catholic was involved in the ownership. However, a great hew and cry went up from the furious religious establishments over burial services performed by non-believers.[14] In 1927, Lauterburg and Oehler moved to the west end of the Hagenbring building. In 1937, they relocated their operation to 111 West Campbell, the present site of the Metropolis Performing Arts Centre. In 1958, they moved yet again to their present location on Northwest Highway.[15]

To bring additional industry and revenue into the village, F.B. Williams, Frank Thurston and John Sigwalt formed a private corporation in 1875 to help Sigwalt relocate his foundry business from Chicago to Arlington Heights. The following year, residents raised $11,000 in cash and real estate to help build Sigwalt's two-story structure on Foundry (now Kensington) Road, so called because the ashes left over from the foundry were scattered on the dirt road in winter to keep wheels, horses and feet from slipping. For the next several years, the Sigwalt Company cast the iron treadles used in Singer sewing machines. Sigwalt was sold to the Diamond Sewing Machine Company in 1883. The factory burned down in 1895 and the ruins were purchased by James Harris to cast gray iron sewing machine parts and seat standards. The business was expanded six years later by George Peter and Albert Volz to produce both school desk and opera seat standards.

During this growth period, a second railroad track was laid, permitting two-way rail traffic. Curiously, the C&NW set up its signals, switches and sidings so that its trains ran in the opposite direction to all other railroads in the United States. It remains today the only "left-hand" running railroad in the country, even though it is now operated by the Union Pacific.

Arlington Heights, Illinois

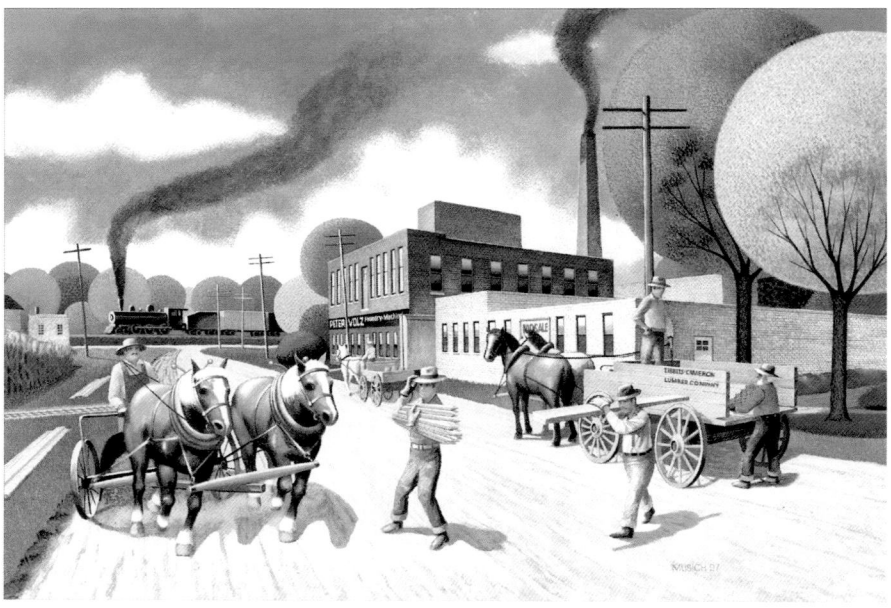

Foundry Road, late 1800s, east of State Road (Arlington Heights Road), at the corner of what is now Northwest Highway. Today, Foundry Road is Kensington Road. The building was the site of the Sigwalt Sewing Machine Company foundry in the late nineteenth century. *Painting by Jack Musich.*

With all this manufacturing and construction brewing in the downtown area, Arlington Heights was saved from becoming a grim factory town choked with ash, manure, soot and cheaply built stores smack up against each other by the plans of the founder. William Dunton had always been a generous donor of land and money for the betterment of his namesake town, but the gifts had strings attached where the village image was concerned. His bequest of land in the center of town stipulated that it must remain a green public park with carriage paths and wide avenues. Once, when the railroad threatened to turn the land into a parking lot, the elderly Dunton countered that he would withdraw his bequest and charge for the property. The tight-fisted railroad backed down. Railroad Park became a buffer between the dusty progress of growth and the civility of elegant country living.

Already, the influx of immigrants to fill the factory jobs had been relegated to the south side of Campbell Street that ran parallel to the tracks. This area was locally referred to as the "Hell Hole" by those Yankees and upscale Germans north of the tracks in the area called "Piety Hill" after the five churches that were clustered near the town center. A few churches remained on the south side, and frequent complaints came from church members who

Growing Up by the Tracks

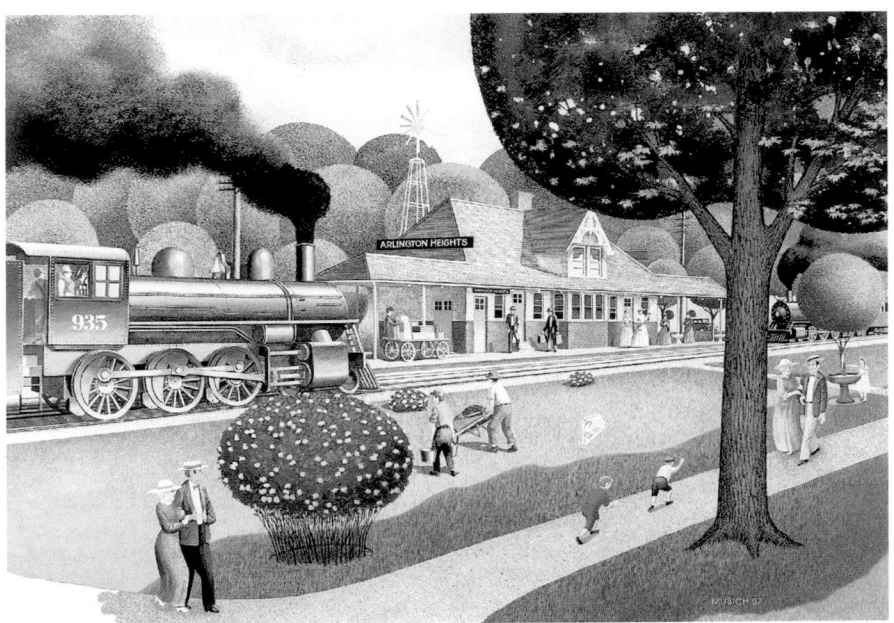

A steam train approaches the Arlington Heights train station and Railroad Park in the foreground, circa 1910. *Painting by Jack Musich.*

had to pass the swinging doors of the saloons on their way to worship and come face to face with the merry workers letting off steam after long shifts over metal stampers and furnaces.

Henry Meyer embraced the situation. In 1883, Henry, together with James Kennicott and Chris Geils, purchased a plot of property near the southwest corner of State Road and the C&NW railroad track, which included a shallow pond. They deepened the pond and diverted two creeks to maintain a level deep enough to freeze over in the winter, which provided ice for sale during the summer. The park bordering the pond and the pavilion on its shore became Arlington Heights landmarks and part of the social center of the village. Boy Scouts, Elks, Red Star, Moose and other organizations rented the facilities for parties, picnics and "socials" of all kinds. The fire department brought out its latest pumper to dip the hose in the pond and demonstrate hose-power. In the summer, the C&NW Railroad boosted its passenger service by offering special tours from hot, reeking Chicago to rural locations. Meyers Pond became one of those destinations.

During the winter, when plunging temperatures and layers of snow had numbed the village, Saturday skating parties made their way to the pond,

Arlington Heights, Illinois

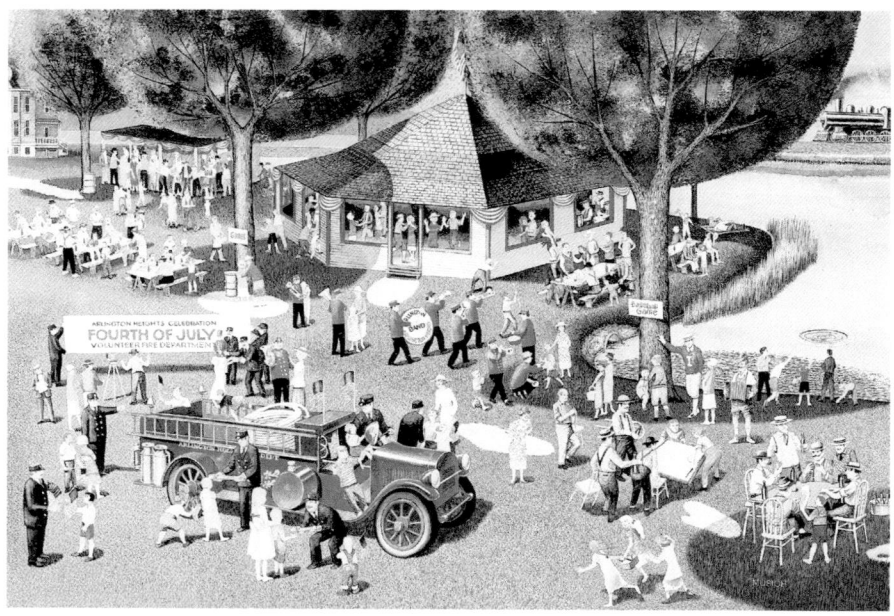

The Fourth of July was celebrated at Meyers Pond, on the southeast side of Arlington Heights Road and Northwest Highway. The pond and its beer garden and dance pavilion operated from the 1880s to 1934. *Painting by Jack Musich.*

some bringing tin "growlers" that held hot cocoa instead of beer, with tin cups looped over the handles. Japanese lanterns reflected off the scarred ice as the skaters carved their way around the pond, stroking and swooping as the chill breeze whipped their trailing scarves and tugged at layers of wool and denim. With the rising moon, the lights were dimmed and the revelers made their way home, each carrying a hand-held kerosene lantern, and the yellow lamps bobbed and coasted along like orderly fireflies to the horses' muffled clip-clop and the crunching trudge of booted feet.

Entertainment in town, while much of it was organized, was also scaled down to a young couple trying to find a place to be together, a family looking to wear out the kids or just an excuse to take an evening "constitutional" after work. Many homes were built with shaded front porches for rocking chairs and gliders. A pitcher of lemonade was often available to pausing strollers. For the more active, bicycle clubs held outings, risking life and limb aboard the tall-wheeled "Ordinaries" that were called "penny-farthings" in England—because of their large front wheel and very small rear wheel—or speeding up and down the risky dirt roads on the smaller "safety bikes," chased by dogs and spooking horses.

Growing Up by the Tracks

Families that could afford them had pianos with benches crammed with sheet music, and there was always someone who could saw a good fiddle, play the spoons or wail on a brassy coronet. With the large German population, bands were numerous and were heavy on the wind instruments. Rehearsals pumping music through the open windows of the Union Hotel's upstairs hall on warm summer evenings were common. Side streets came alive as curtains fluttered, while inside, stand-up music boxes rotated large tin discs studded with pegs that tripped tiny hammers playing the tunes of the time.

Dunton was a small farm town without a scrap of anonymity. Everyone knew everyone else. If a family took the train into Chicago or visited friends in East Wheeling, that was news. When the village consisted of only a few shops and the Union Hotel, news of the outside world arrived from Chicago in stacks of newspapers dropped off the northbound train and from publications such as *Harper's Weekly*. As populations grew, a local voice was needed for the printed page. In 1872, G.E. Sarlie started up the *Cook County Herald*, a four-page newspaper printed in neighboring Palatine. In addition to local comings and goings, meetings and birthdays, cattle sales and auctions, he needed news items cribbed from the Chicago papers to fill his weekly four pages. He expanded to the *Palatine Herald* in 1873 and then sold both papers, which changed hands until George Bugbee acquired the *Cook County Herald* and the retitled *Palatine Enterprise*.

While these papers battled for advertising and news in the northwest communities, farther north, Hosea Christian Paddock recovered from a major fire that had wiped out his *Lake County Independent*, published in Libertyville, Illinois. He brought the thirst for knowledge of a schoolteacher and a shrewd sales sense to the local newspaper scene when he borrowed $175 to buy the *Palatine Herald* and then another $275 to pick up the *Cook County Herald* in 1899. To corner the news market, he then bought the *Palatine Enterprise* as well.

H.C. brought his son Stuart into the business to help produce the *Enterprise*, which was peeled off a two-page hand press that required two people to haul down on the lever, pushing and pulling the inked plates to produce three hundred copies. Getting a newspaper on the streets in those nineteenth-century days was a formidable task. Once the news and advertising was gathered by reporters and salesmen at an office at the corner of Vail Avenue and Campbell Street, the copy had to be translated into printing type. This was done in Palatine on a "linotype" machine that turned molten lead into lines of hot type called "slugs" that were keyed into a box called a "chase" with headlines and ruled lines to separate the stories. These chases with lead versions of each page were locked and sent by train to the sheet-fed press in

41

Arlington Heights, Illinois

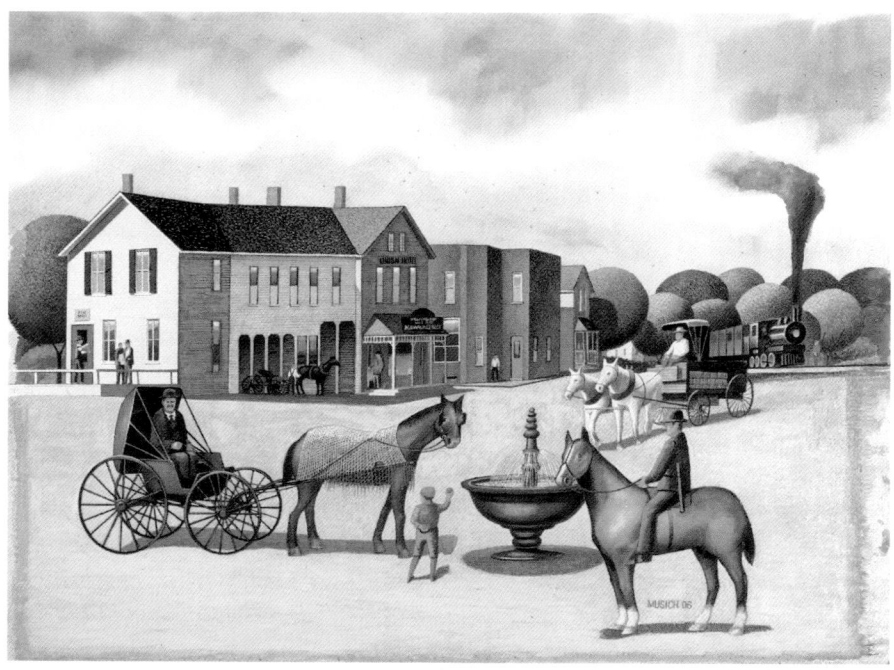

A horse watering fountain, possibly at the corner of Davis Street and Dunton Avenue. *Painting by Jack Musich.*

Chicago. Eventually, as subscriptions and over-the-counter sales grew, the hot-type chases were pressed into mattes that could conform to the cylinder high-speed presses as used on modern papers today.

The Paddocks purchased a three-story frame building at 15 West Davis Street at a cost of $1,200 in 1904. In keeping with the need for more editions to serve surrounding communities, they bought a gasoline engine and powered their own printing press. Soon, the *Herald* newspapers were showing up in Niles Center, Shermerville, Glenview, Morton Grove, Norwood Park and Franklin Park. Hosea Paddock saw to some of the home distribution hands-on as he climbed aboard his wagon pulled by his patient horse, Bonnie, and toured the back roads in search of new subscriptions and bits of news to fill his many pages. Later, he upgraded to a one-cylinder Holsman automobile. Often, he also returned with a bushel of apples, fresh eggs or other goods in lieu of hard cash, which was not as common as barter in the more outlying areas. H.C. Paddock and Sons built a newspaper empire that survived the Great Depression and continued on into the digital age, always with the motto on the front page: "To fear God, tell the truth and make money."[16]

Chapter 3

EDUCATION AND WORSHIP COME TO ARLINGTON HEIGHTS

By the late nineteenth century, aside from commerce and transportation, two driving forces shaped most rural communities in the Midwest: education and worship. Neither of these was as important as food, clothing and shelter, but commitment to them rounded off the rough edges of prairie life and survival. The farmers and shopkeepers who settled Arlington Heights and the immigrants from Europe who followed were not the huddled masses who packed into the big cities looking for any labor to feed and care for their families. Arlington Heights's founders and early residents wanted to own the ground they lived on and brought the kind of ambition that followed America's westward expansion.

But prairie life was hard, dirty and brutal. Food had to be grown or slaughtered. Shelter had to be carved from wood and chiseled from stone. Cloth for clothing was coarse and bolts of linen were difficult to come by. Farm families were large because it took many hands to drag life out of a plot of ground. Children died young from dysentery, colic, pneumonia, accidents in the field, scalding and scourges of diphtheria and smallpox. Most youngsters were home-schooled when there was time, because chores always came first. They learned from the one book that usually traveled with the family, the Bible, or another religious text, often in a language other than English.

Two buildings that a village must contain provide the civilized backbone for that community: a school and a place of worship. With the coming of the railroad, shops, roads and commerce, the society of other residents followed. Knowing how to read and write in English stripped away isolation. It became necessary for the collection of buildings and farms to become a working village in Cook County. Education was a necessity and families had to adapt.

Arlington Heights, Illinois

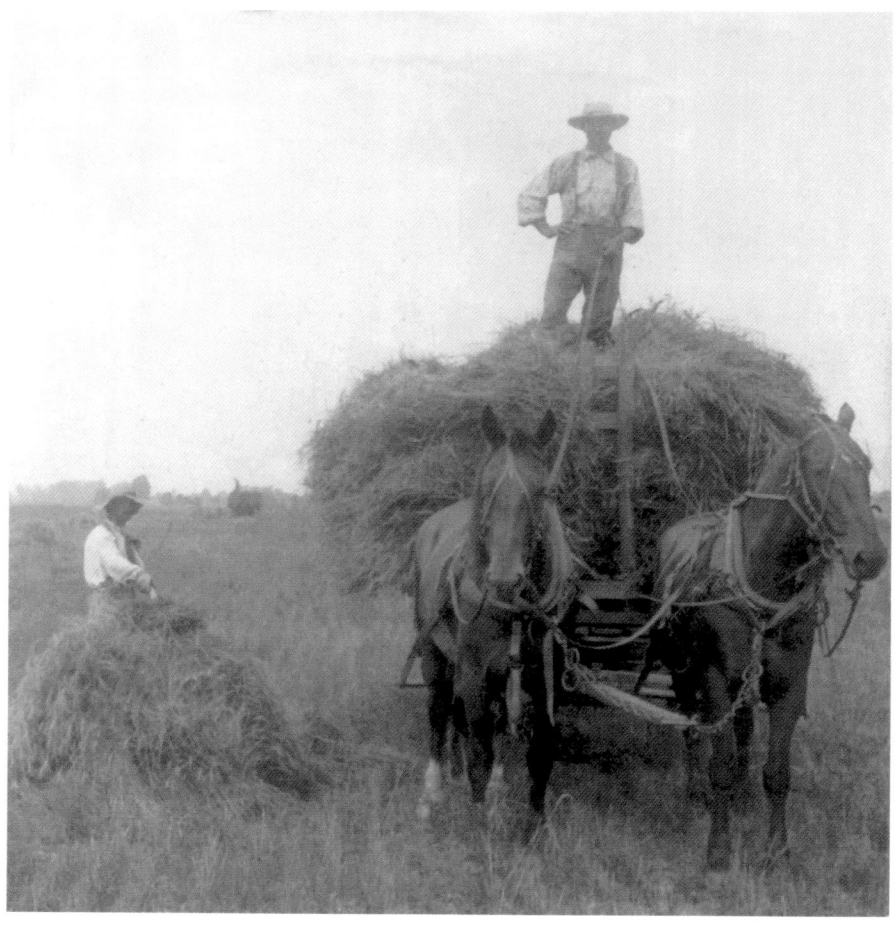

A farmer on a hay wagon, late nineteenth century. Arlington Heights was a farming community up to the early 1960s. *Courtesy of the Library of Congress.*

Of course, every community endeavor begins small. In 1849, before the railroad arrived and when most of downtown was still unsold land, West Wheeling (soon to be Dunton) opened its first school. Small by any standard, the sixteen- by sixteen-foot square box opened to a single class—all ages—of ten students. A bench ran around three of the inside walls. The teacher, a game and versatile instructor named Miss Sarah Thornton, had a desk for herself, a chair, a longer desk and a stove that burned wood and, later, coal. For lessons, the children learned writing with chalk on erasable slates or with pencils, making sure to use both sides of the precious paper. This educational system served for several years at the corner of Miner Street and Evergreen Avenue.

Education and Worship Come to Arlington Heights

Enrollment grew, and by the late 1800s, the school had expanded to two rooms. In 1870, a brick building costing $10,000 was constructed with four rooms presided over by three teachers. By this time, School District 10 had been organized as well. As for books, paper, ink and payment for the teachers, the community had to foot those bills through taxes. The classrooms did not house separate grade levels, but were divided into multi-age classes. A census taken in 1884 shows that there were about five hundred persons under the age of twenty-one living in the village, and it is estimated that about half of those were enrolled in the Lutheran School sponsored by St. Peter's Church. Lutherans made up the bulk of Arlington Heights's German population.

The teachers were single ladies: Miss Lucy Hart, Miss Kunie Horcher, Miss Evans and Miss Lydia Lorenzen—who was a widow—with Mr. Nathaniel Banta acting as principal. Working teachers were required to board with community families, as were nurses and other "career" women. Education was also gender related. For boys, it was necessary to step up and take their place in the world of business and letters; for women, not so much. Their place in society as mothers and housewives was preordained. Their skills they could learn at home or, if there was enough money, at special schools for girls that taught domestic and social sciences.

While Arlington Heights's schools taught students from the first through eighth grade, any youngster who wished to move on to high school had to take the train in to Chicago or go to the school in Maine Township.

The need for a place of worship came early. In 1855, shortly after the railroad arrived, a group of citizens held a community meeting in William Dunton's barn and formed the first religious society in the village. They comprised a mixed bag of denominations, and during one of their meetings at Socrates Rand's store on Rand Road in Des Plaines, they decided to join the Presbyterian Church and ask for support from that organization. The following year, the First Presbyterian Church was built of wood and shingles at the corner of Eastman and Dunton Avenues. It became both a social and religious center until 1911, when it was moved to become a gymnasium and later an apartment building.

Methodists arrived in Dunton in 1860 and established their church at the corner of St. James Street and Dunton Road. This Colonial-style building brought combined congregations in the area closer to the railroad to allow for the coming population growth. Lutherans built their church in 1860 on Evergreen Street just south of Sigwalt Avenue and eventually ended up in a new brick building—built by members of the congregation—40 feet by 70 feet in size beneath a 110-foot spire. The Lutherans were great builders and a close community. They converted the old unused Universalist church into

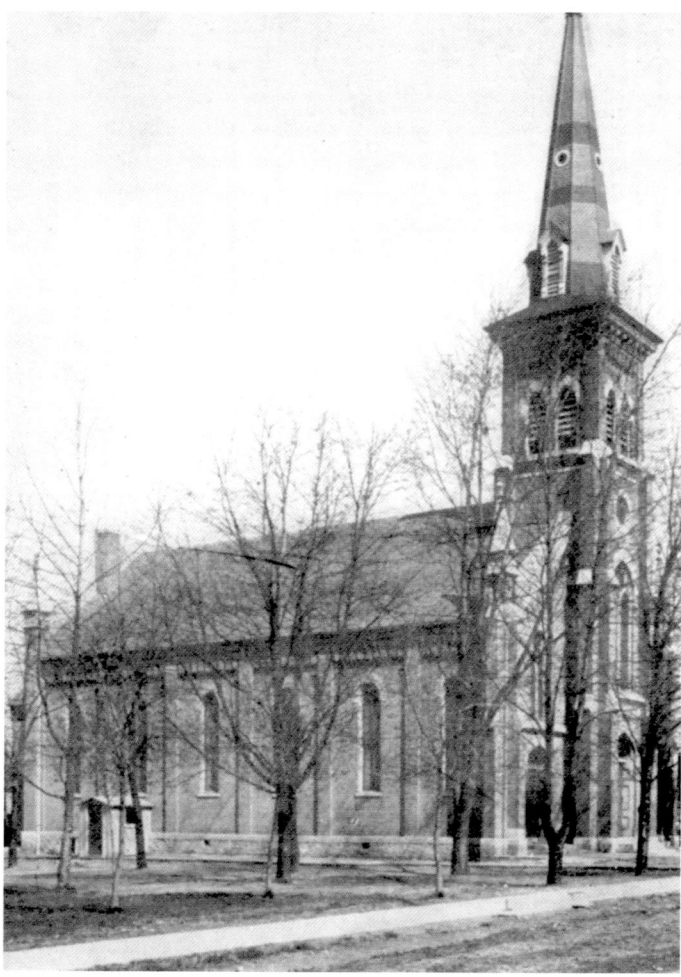

St. Peter's Lutheran Church on Northwest Highway. In the late 1950s, the school and church were torn down and rebuilt on Olive Street. *Courtesy of Donna Turek.*

a parochial school and then, in 1899, built a new brick school named St. Peter's. They sold the old Universalist church, which was moved to 402–404 North Chestnut Street. Their construction projects extended to their senior citizens as well when, in 1892, they created the Altenheim Home for the Aged on Walnut Street between Euclid Avenue and what became Northwest Highway. Besides residences, the property also provided a large garden plot—cared for by the residents—to grow its own vegetables.

There is one notable point made obvious in the above narrative about early architecture in Arlington Heights. It was truly a "movable feast" for historians. As opposed to today's "tear-downs" suddenly vanishing overnight in a train of dump trucks, nineteenth- and early twentieth-

Education and Worship Come to Arlington Heights

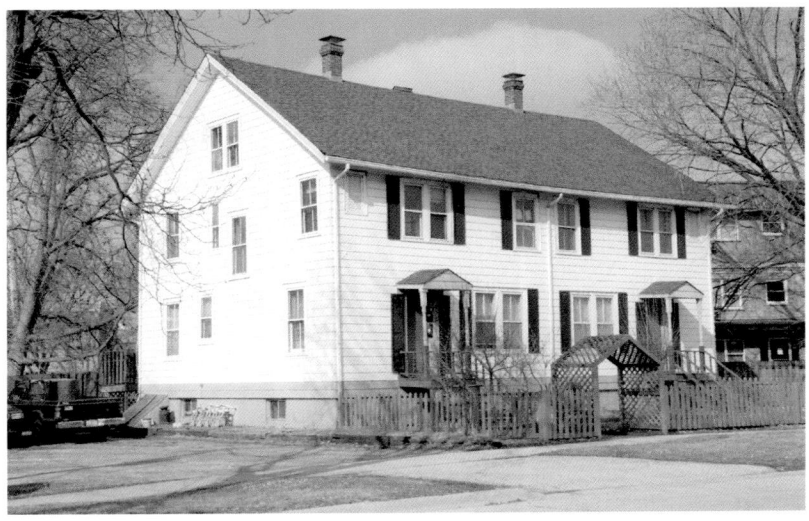

Number 402–404 North Chestnut. This private house became apartments after being moved to this location from three other addresses where it had served as a church and a parochial school. *Photo by Gerry Souter.*

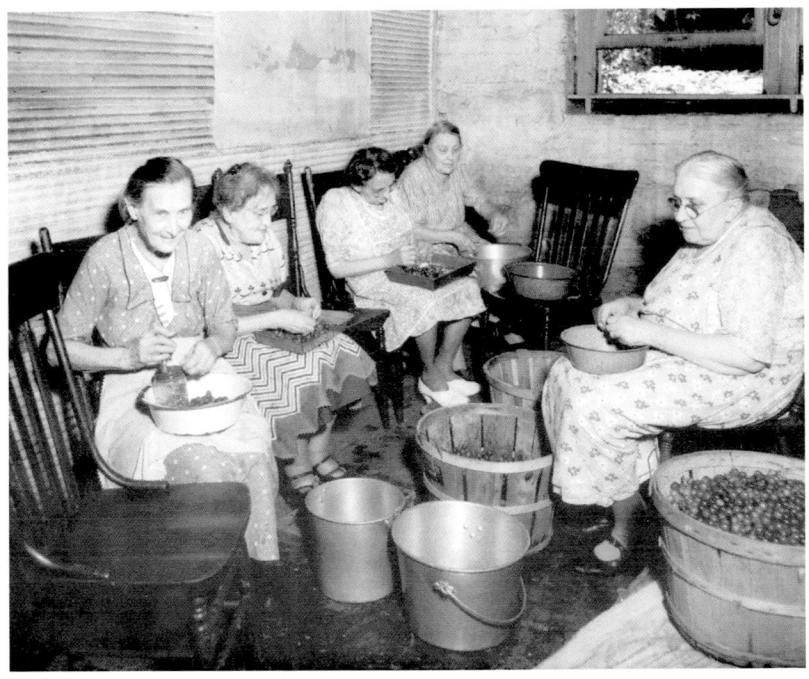

Ladies pitting cherries, Lutheran Home, 1940s. *Courtesy of Donna Turek.*

century construction was loaded up on wheels and moved about. Peripatetic churches seemed to lead the parade.

According to architect Tom Seibert, the Elk Grove Methodist Church at Arlington Heights and Algonquin Roads was moved twice in the late 1800s because of noise from nearby taverns. The Lutherans moved the original Universalist church from its foundation at Vail and St. James Streets to a Chestnut Street location, and later to 407 North Vail. The Presbyterians' original church building ended up at Vail Avenue and Vine Street. As the building was en route to its new location one Sunday, services continued to be held. Another place of worship, a Catholic church, was uprooted and shipped by rail to the town of Des Plaines, about ten miles away.

The religion by rail tale doesn't end here. Margery Frisbie, Arlington Heights historian, discovered this brief addendum. Some Catholic parishioners missed hearing Mass and other rituals once the little church was gone. In Des Plaines, Father John Linden volunteered to help. Northwest Highway had not yet been built between the two towns, so the priest commandeered a handcar from the railroad and pumped himself down the tracks to Arlington Heights to say Mass on the second floor of Temperance Hall. He made the trip once a week, heard confessions, instructed the children, stayed overnight in the home of a parishioner and then hopped aboard his handcar and pumped back to Des Plaines in time for the late Mass.

On peaceful afternoons, churches, homes and schools could be seen serenely coasting down Arlington Heights Streets, rumbling through town to their next life.[17]

Chapter 4

FIRE, POLICE AND PLUMBING

Everyone who lived on the windswept prairie had a healthy respect for fire. In 1871, half the townspeople had climbed on village rooftops to watch the hellish flames devour Chicago from south to north. And then there had been the blaze that destroyed two village stores in 1875, resulting in brick construction replacing clapboard structures. Dry summers turned dwellings into tinder boxes, and homes were still lit and warmed by open flames. But for the first fifty-six years of growth and development, Arlington Heights had no firefighting organization or equipment. There were no street hydrants, only individual wells and cisterns. Access to water in town was from private well-heads and the town water fountain, which cost residents two dollars a year to use for their horses. Float pumps kept other horse troughs and backyard cisterns filled. Weller Creek and Meyers Pond were water sources, but getting the water to the fire required volunteer bucket brigades. Every shop owner was required to keep a bucket handy just for that purpose.

In 1894, Charles Sigwalt, the Civil War diarist, had been elected Arlington Heights village president, a position that he served off and on until 1905. He called a meeting of the village board on October 8 to establish a volunteer fire department. Wheeled out onto the street was the first piece of firefighting equipment, a Howe hand pumper named "Old Faithful," purchased for $650, including fifteen feet of suction hose and one hundred feet of rope. The fire engine was designed to be pulled by a team of horses, or ten men between the shafts. Water was carried on board in a wood stave barrel laid horizontal in the wagon bed. A pair of parallel wood poles attached to the pump arms could be pulled down to either side of the fire engine and manned five men to a side. Water was drawn into the pump chamber on the up stroke and forced out through the hose on the down stroke. Old Faithful's barrel cistern was kept full by drawing water from a well or creek through the suction hose with a screen filter on the end to keep out weeds, frogs and small fish.

Thirty-seven names were accepted and added to the new volunteer fire department. The second floor of the village hall was furnished with twenty-four chairs, two tables and oil lamps as a clubroom for the volunteers, and twenty-four keys were issued. Each fireman paid fifteen cents a year to cover the janitor's salary. In March 1894, a fire bell was purchased for $30 and a wheeled hose cart for $105. The expenditure of $20 was approved for seven hundred feet of hose. Ten rubber coats, pairs of boots and axes rounded out the basic outfitting. To add water sources to the vulnerable downtown business district, two storm sewer cisterns were built and buried, at the corner of Dunton and Campbell and over on State Road, to act as reservoirs for Old Faithful filled by road seepage. Another well was dug in 1895 that delivered forty gallons a minute.

As with most volunteer fire departments, it did not take long for a certain "elitism" to saturate these rugged fellows who were the protectors of village property and lives. Snappy uniforms were ordered and membership became such a mark of distinction that the smoke-eaters wore their blue shirts trimmed in white insignia, black hats, red belts and black ties to non-fire department–related functions. That practice was squelched by the village board.

Competition also flared in the ranks. The nature of a volunteer department required the men to leave their jobs at the ringing of the fire bell—and, later, the telephone—rush to the firehouse, man the fire engine, hose cart and a chemical cart on wheels and dash off to extinguish the fire. Louie Clark and Fred Binder harnessed their respective teams of horses and would sprint for the firehouse. The first to arrive got to hitch up to Old Faithful and take home an extra two-dollar payment. After some disputes over who arrived first, Louie got the full-time job. Eventually, his horses became so accustomed to the fire alarm that they pounded off toward the fire without waiting for a driver, with the bully boys of the fire brigade in hot pursuit.[18]

To generate revenue, in 1895 the Illinois General Assembly decreed that all fire insurance companies selling policies had to contribute 2 percent of all premiums collected to the local fire department.[19] That same year, the Diamond Sewing Machine Company on Foundry Street was gutted by fire, but its brick construction and prompt action by the Arlington Heights Fire Department kept the flames from spreading.

Protection of property and individuals also included the maintenance of law and order. When the village of Arlington Heights was officially incorporated on February 8, 1887, elections were held and appointments were made. High on the list was that of village constable. The first peace

Fire, Police and Plumbing

officer appointed to patrol the village was James McLaughlin. This stalwart constable received no salary but was allowed to keep 10 percent of all the dog license taxes he could collect at one dollar per dog. He also received fifty cents for every unlicensed dog he captured and dispatched. The town lamplighter, whose work began as the sun set, told the *Cook County Herald* that he "never saw the watchman" after dark. Apparently, dogs were easier to catch in broad daylight. People kept an eye on their pooches in those days.

While Arlington Heights was hardly a hotbed of crime, the police department, such as it was, had a responsibility to generate revenue from fines. Before the automobile arrived and the village became a notorious speed trap for unwary "automobilists," crimes tended to be misdemeanors and acts of domestic abuse. The misdemeanors included swearing and/or rude conduct in or near any church or school, tying a horse to any fence or tree without the owner's permission and dumping garbage or manure that might obstruct passage on the streets or sidewalks. Public drunkenness was too common even to get written up, unless the imbiber became abusive.

The following year saw the village board "Jail Committee" still bogged down in creating a place to hold miscreants awaiting trial and sticky-fingered tramps passing through. The village board did pony up $1.50 to cover the cost of a badge for Constable McLaughlin. Until 1892, the board had been quite peripatetic, holding meetings wherever space could be found. But that year, it purchased the use of a commercial building at the corner of Wing and Davis Streets for a village hall. The main meeting room was approved for trials in 1893, and the jail problem could no longer be put off. Two cells were purchased: one five by seven feet and the other six by seven feet in size. Criminals were moved into the basement and were provided with blankets and bunks. Since the basement was unheated, the village crime rate plummeted in the winter. No act of debauchery was worth spending a night in that dank, frozen cell.

Unfortunately, the only entrance to the basement cell block was through the trial chambers. The decorum of the court suffered greatly when drunken tosspots, soiled tramps, snarling wife beaters and other shackled prisoners were dragged through whatever proceedings had been gaveled to order.

About 1900, the police force expanded and officers were provided with uniforms, domed hats, whistles to call for aid and sand-filled, lead-weighted saps when order could only be restored with a tap on the noggin. The German farmers had great respect for the German police officers and usually the flash of a badge settled all disputes. With this authority came the responsibility to see that the sidewalks were shoveled in the winter and that board members leaving the Wheeling House with a snoot full of who-hit-john got home safely.

Arlington Heights, Illinois

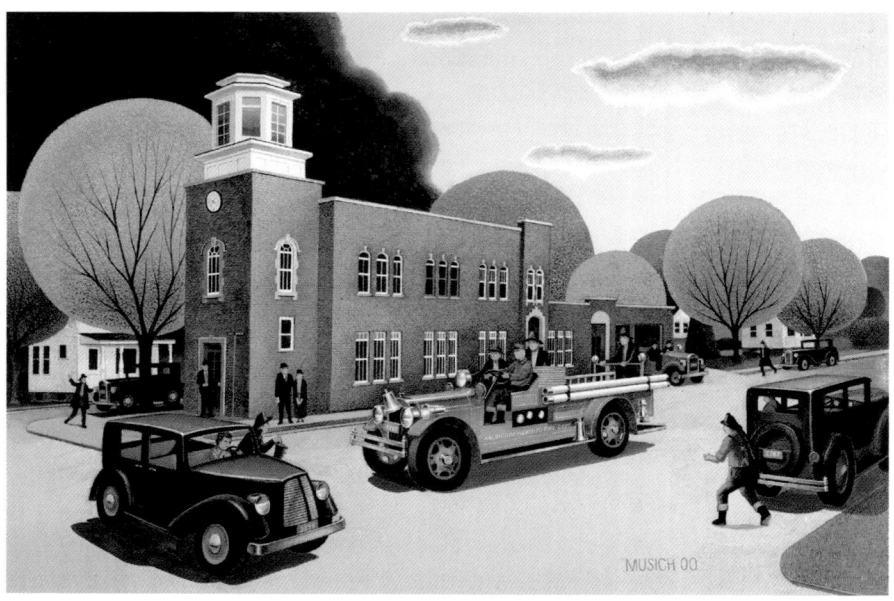

Village hall, 1930. The building was constructed on the triangle of Wing Street, Vail Avenue and Davis Street as a one-story structure in 1913, housing village offices, the police department and the fire department. Village business was conducted there until 1962, when the new municipal building at Arlington Heights Road and Sigwalt was dedicated. *Painting by Jack Musich.*

Arthur Dieball, hired in 1906, was the first fully outfitted police officer. He was described in the pages of the *Cook County Herald* as a "fearless young man who carries the dignity of the law with the able assistance of Constable McNab and Marshall (Henry) Horstman." The addition of this defender of justice caused the *Herald* to further rhapsodize, "Evil-doers will have to give the Heights a wide berth, or languish behind bars in the village Bastille." Sadly, Dieball's tenure was brief due to a growing family (ten kids) and the miserly pay. He went to work for the C&NW at the Clinton Street Yards. The word must have gotten out. Within a year of his departure, an evildoer stuck up the Pure Oil station in town and made off with the day's receipts to become the first armed robber recorded by the village.[20]

Also, the new century finally introduced the horseless carriage to the rugged streets and gravel roads of Arlington Heights. A speed limit of six miles per hour was imposed and failure to sufficiently warn pedestrians and citizens with horses of the machine's approach was also subject to a fine. The *Whoompah!* of bulb horns became common in the village.

Fire, Police and Plumbing

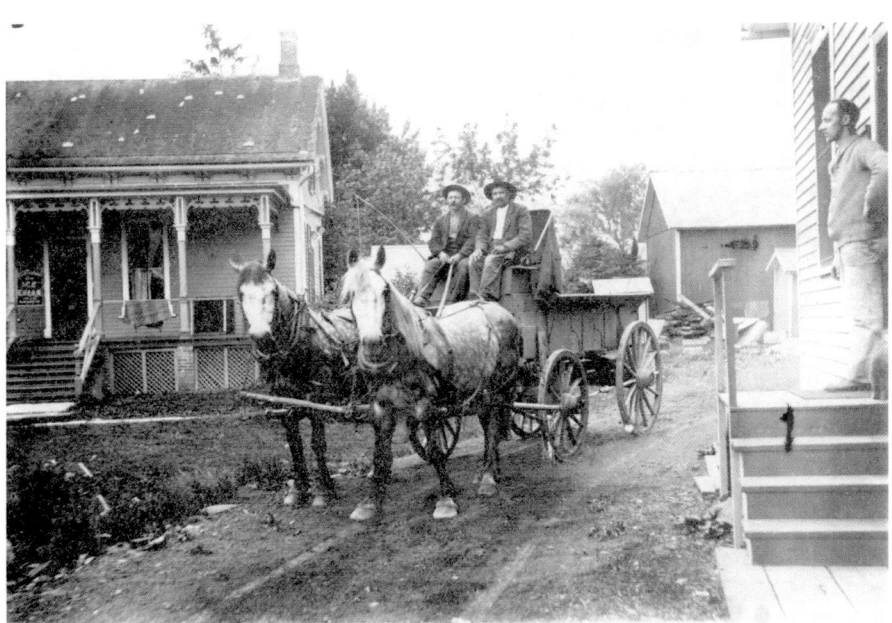

Fred Gieseke (in the wagon on the right) drives his wagon along the alley that opened onto the south side of Campbell Street, just east of Highland, circa 1910. He owned a farmhouse that faced Highland. To the left is a clapboard building that later became a funeral home and is now the site of the Metropolis Performing Arts Centre. *Courtesy of Donna Turek.*

Early vehicles of the 1900s, such as the REO and curved dash Oldsmobile, buggy-type cars seating two people above a one- or two-cylinder engine, were hardly threats to life and limb except when a backfire set a panicked horse careening through town. Gasoline was bought from a barrel with a spigot at the hardware store and filtered through a cheesecloth to keep drowned flies and moths out of the carburetor. In the country, the growth of the car culture was moved along smartly by the kids. Stephen Urick, an octogenarian, remembered to historian Margery Frisbie:

> *You could buy a car that could run for $5 or $10. When three or four of us kids got together, we would play car tag. We'd chase each other up and down streets which had utilities in, but no houses yet. Sometimes we'd even ride up over the curb to cross a block and catch another car. You could be 12 years old driving a car. Other local show-offs sat on top of the back seat and drove with their feet, "Look, Ma, no hands!"*[21]

If this kind of behavior kept the phone ringing at the police station, it also served another cause, though the process took some time. More horseless carriages meant fewer horses and their associated effluvia. On a warm summer day with no breeze during the horse era, downtown Arlington Heights could be overwhelming. Added to the horse problem was the natural watershed that drained northwest to southeast through an open ditch to Meyers Pond and then under the railroad and into Weller Creek. This eight-foot-wide ditch had become a dumping ground for garbage of all sorts, including dead animals. Typhoid fever had become rampant and rats thrived on the refuse. Water from this natural runoff was gathering in home and shop owners' basements.

The village board decided to move the watershed underground via a brick sewer and drew up plans in 1902. No special assessment could be made and bonds were not issued to pay for the work and materials. Only by cutting spending and keeping a sharp eye on budgets was the job completed. An engineer agreed to supervise the project for a price not to exceed $200 and the best price of cement ($0.60 a barrel), sand ($1.10 a yard) and brick at $6 per thousand. The sewer project was completed at a cost of $2,500. Twenty years later, when a new sewer system was installed, the original brick tunnels were found to be as sound as ever.[22]

If getting rid of water was a problem, making use of water was equally vexing. The Diamond Sewing Machine fire in 1895 had required the use of tin milk cans carried over from Bray and Kates and filled with water to keep Old Faithful topped up and douse the flames. At best, the blaze was "contained." As the new sewer was being created, the village board decided that now was the time to build a public water works, not only for the fire department, but also to provide running water in residents' homes and places of business.

The well pump out back was as familiar to Arlington Heights architecture as was the often elaborate outhouse with a crate of corncobs inside or an old Sears Roebuck catalogue. Pumps had to be primed with a few strokes of the lever or turns of the chain crank to start the water flow. Indoor water required pressure to come out of the sink tap at the twist of a handle. Pumps froze in the winter and had to be busted loose or heated with a blowtorch. The water was always cold, requiring a tin or iron cistern attached to the stove to be filled and heated.

To achieve that water pressure—and butting heads against considerable tight-fisted opposition—the village board earmarked $10,000 from the general fund. E.P. Mueller stepped forward to donate two lots on which to construct a raised tank. This tank lofted 125 feet above the business district

Fire, Police and Plumbing

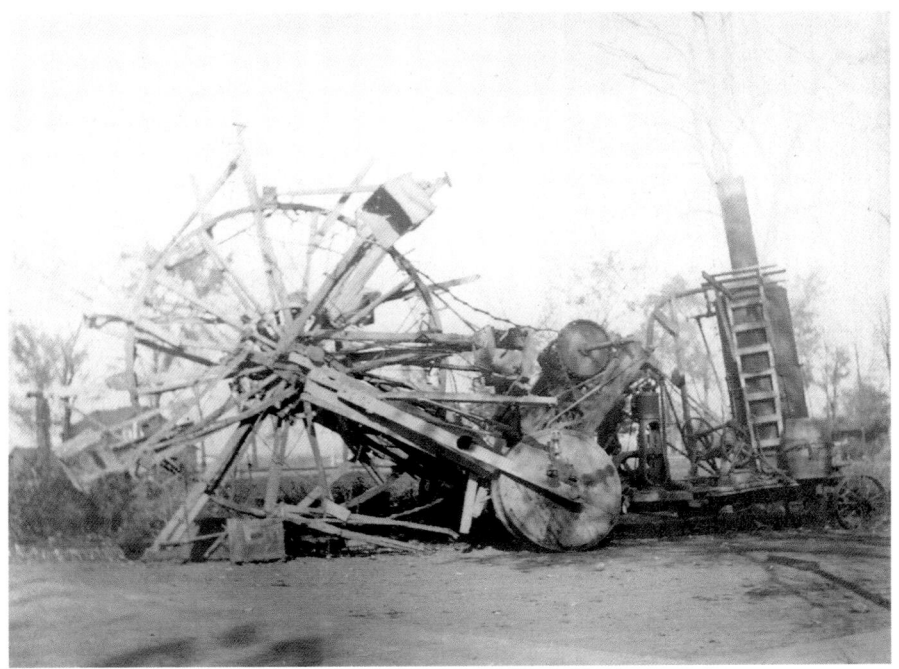

A sewer digger, 1928. This was used by the Arlington Heights village services to dig ground for storm and sanitary sewers. It was built in 1928–29. *Courtesy of the Arlington Heights Historical Society.*

and was tapped into an artesian well 14 feet below ground. Water would then be available to thirty thousand Arlington residents. Two steam pumps were added, along with a storage reservoir, and mains were piped to the corners of the village as it existed in 1902 to 1905, the duration of the project.[23]

Just five years later, the final step to bringing big-city civilization to the rural farm town astride the railroad tracks was begun. In 1910, while indoor plumbing was available, it was up to the private owner to provide a septic tank, which took up a considerable part of the backyard. Once again, the village board girded for battle and authorized the drawing of plans for a sewer system and the building of a village septic tank. Two years of political and economic infighting finally resulted in two engineering firms agreeing on a combined effort, and in 1912 all the connections were made. An Arlington Heights family could flush with confidence.[24]

Chapter 5

ARLINGTON HEIGHTS MARCHES OFF TO WAR

By the turn of the century, Arlington Heights had shed much of its farm town baggage and emerged into the new twentieth century as a modernized work in progress. While the roads were still a gumbo of muck after every rain, Euclid Avenue now wore a layer of graded gravel. In town, through great effort and busy screw jacks, most of the shops had been lifted as much as four feet above the ooze. Plank sidewalks and flights of wood and iron steps guaranteed that a shopper or businessman stayed dry shod during any downtown journey.

The key to progress was improved roads. Developers were buying up lots on which to build single-family homes, which required side streets to connect to the town center. While most people still rode in buggies or wagons or astride horses, larger, more powerful automobiles that held up to six people, along with hard-sprung trucks, began chattering and chugging through the business district. Automobilists from Chicago ventured out into the hinterlands and many turned down Foundry or Euclid from Rand Road to see Arlington Heights. Meyers Pond was a natural draw for auto tourists. Train commuters passing through the village often returned as more services became available. The quality of life was still relatively bucolic and farm service oriented, but as transportation improved, a new breed of city types took up residence.

They appeared in the early morning, gathering on the train station platform with the salesmen who had spent the night at the Union. These were not farm family types whose clothes were a year or two behind fashion and who had a couple of kids in knickers or second-best dresses hanging on, excited about the impending adventure. No, these single adults were fashionable "commuters" who lived in Arlington Heights and worked in Chicago. Train schedules had been expanded to include these daily travelers.

Arlington Heights, Illinois

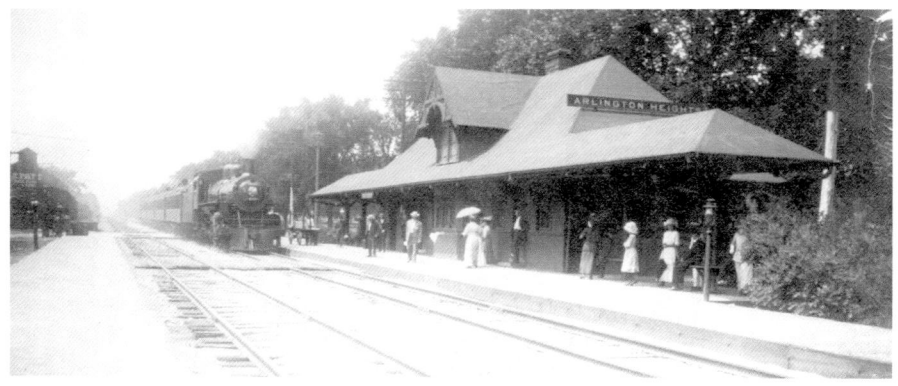

Arlington Heights train station, circa 1915. This depot was built on the north side of the track in 1892. The new station also boasted wide parkways for buggies to unload on either side of the tracks. *Courtesy of the Arlington Heights Historical Society.*

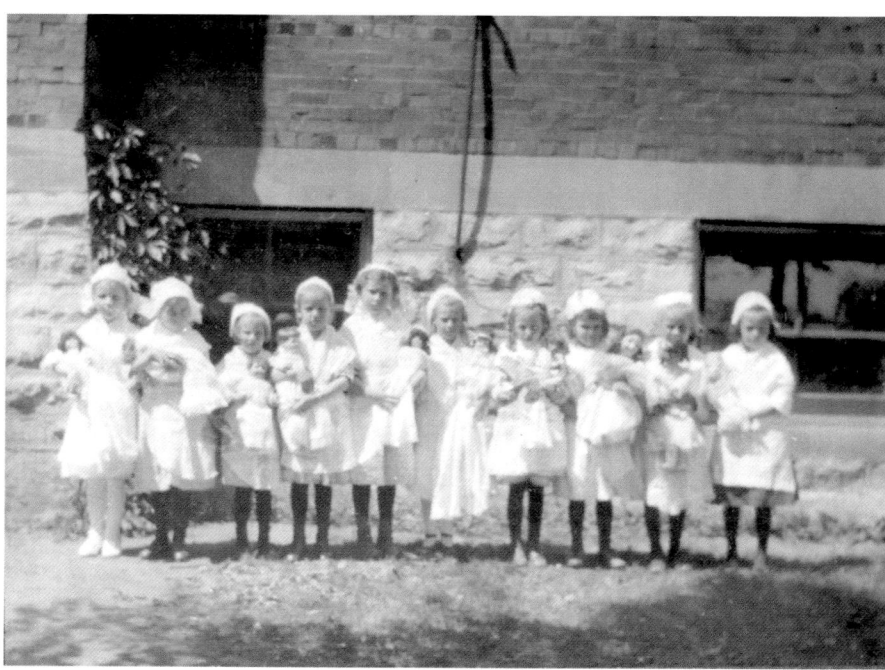

Kindergarten girls, circa 1913. *From left*: Rosalie Horcher, Margaret Johnson, Aurelia Rau, Wilhemina Mueller, Laura Dieball, Norma Wilke, Lillian Klehm, Helen Leark, Florence Schad and Gertrude Fitzpatrick. *Courtesy of Donna Turek.*

Arlington Heights Marches Off to War

In the winter, they left lanterns with the stationmaster for their return trip after dark. Many new homes were not yet reached by the latest village gas lighting. The commuters carried newspapers—in English and in German—folded in their overcoat pockets. Those familiar with train travel and the need to present a neat appearance at work always wore overcoats or long cotton dusters in the summer. As the locomotive chugged and clanked into the station, puffing coal soot from its stack, huffing steam from the cylinder cocks and exhaling a film of oil from the air brake compressors, any covering became a good investment.

These commuters, who built their homes well back from the roads and planted front lawns of grass in the East Coast fashion, laid out $600 for Ford automobiles they drove only on weekends and embraced indoor plumbing. They began slowly changing the character of the village. One of those changes affected businesses that had served residents since the mid-nineteenth century. At first, livery stable owners laughed when an automobile needed to be hauled from a ditch by a stout pair of Percheron draft horses. Blacksmiths chuckled when they heated their antique forges to repair an auto clutch or a snapped axel. These tradesmen, who were village fixtures, thought this "progress" was amusing. But autos did not turn expensive feed into dreary piles at the end of a trip, nor did they shy from loud noises. Blacksmiths found themselves becoming mechanical veterinarians to the automobile, which was hardly a perfect machine. But with its persnickety operating idiosyncrasies, it became a profitable invention. Both Arlington Heights blacksmiths, Andrew Horcher and Charlie Peterson, closed their shops to become mechanics and car salesmen. The last blacksmith shop, belonging to Julius Flentie, closed in 1927. He became a politician.

Bit by bit, Arlington Heights was losing its isolation from the world. First it was the roads and then the railroad, followed by automobiles, and by 1900, the telephone had snaked along the tracks from Chicago and a line was dropped into the village. A telephone exchange manned by three operators and a supervisor was set up in the rear of Burkitt's Jewelry store at 11 East Davis. By 1905, there were fifteen subscribers. Imagine having the telephone number "6."

The world flooded in every time the train came through with the mail. Letters poured out grief and hardship as families in Germany told their American cousins about the Great War that had been killing a generation of Europeans since 1914. By 1917, food was in short supply, riots were breaking out and more young German men were being herded into the army to fill the trenches. Finally, in 1917, the newspapers brought word of two incidents: the sinking by a German submarine of the passenger liner

Arlington Heights, Illinois

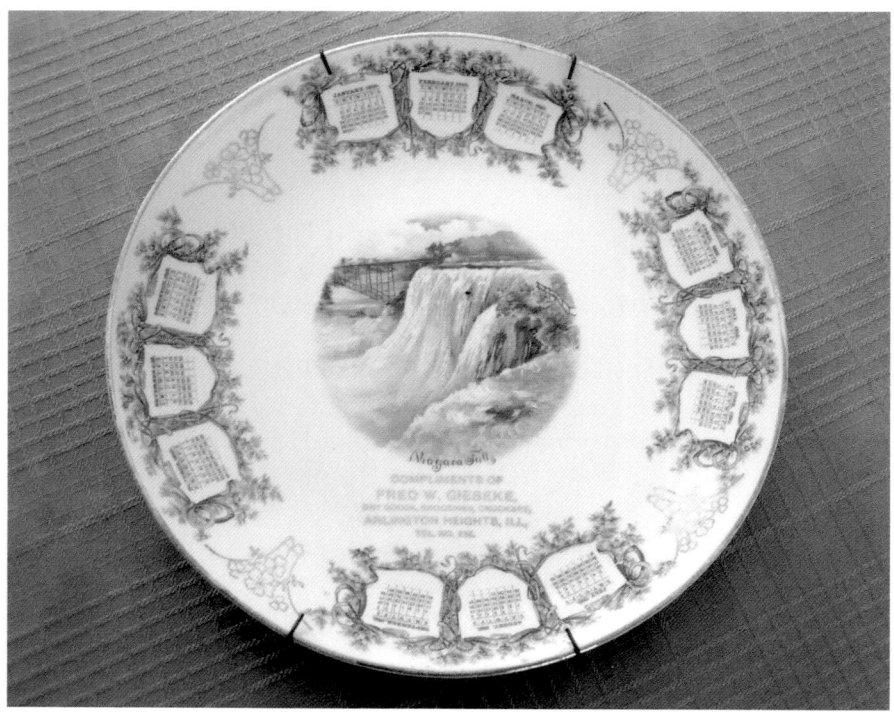

A commemorative plate given to customers as a premium by the Gieseke store. This one is from 1910. *Courtesy of Donna Turek.*

Lusitania with Americans onboard, and the Zimmerman telegram from a German diplomat to the Mexican ambassador. The wire suggested that Mexico retake American lands stolen from it in the 1840s and pledged German assistance. President Woodrow Wilson declared war on Germany and its allies on April 6, 1917.

Suddenly, the Great War was at Arlington Heights's doorstep. The Selective Service Act was created on May 19, calling up able-bodied men and boys between the ages of eighteen and thirty for active military service. City life had taken its toll on the health of American youth and many were found to be unfit for duty. The age spread was increased to forty-five to fill quotas. That was not the case with country youth raised in the rugged rural farm life who grew up in and around Arlington Heights. If there was a problem for community residents, it was caused by propaganda.

In the years preceding America's entry into the war, Great Britain had created a series of staged and highly emotional silent film newsreels. These productions were designed to enflame patriotism and called upon the world

Arlington Heights Marches Off to War

to end the "Hun Scourge." Titles such as *Jelicoe's Grand Fleet* and *Kitchener's Grand Army* showed Britain's might, while *The Battle of the Somme* revealed the horrors of the Hun soldiers bayoneting wounded Allies. Passions against anything German were sometimes violent in Chicago neighborhoods. Hot dogs and dachshunds became "Liberty Pups." Sauerkraut was renamed "Liberty Cabbage."

Because of Arlington Heights's large assimilated population of Germans, life pretty much continued as usual. The German farmers and shopkeepers were second- and third-generation residents and hated the idea of their mother country being under the heel of Kaiser Wilhelm. He represented everything from which their immigrant relatives had fled to start a new life. The *Cook County Herald* continued to publish its German-language edition. While in Chicago a German man was dragged from his home and lynched, an Arlington Heights citizen was featured in the news: "Fred Wulff is a good American citizen, but we believe he holds the record for having the most relatives in the German army. He has 28 relatives in active service."

Sieburg's Drug Store became the hangout to learn news of the war as soldiers home on leave gravitated there to tell their stories. Customers also heard of labor riots happening throughout the country as the government issued many draconian edicts demanding greater efforts in a war economy. Fearing the lack of troops at home to be used to keep the peace, states created militias from younger and older men. The Illinois Volunteer Training Corps donned khakis and drilled with old rifles in the school playground to be available for riot duty. Arlington Heights assembled a company of fifty men and boys under arms. All the Home Guard troops received honorable discharges at the end of the war.

With their young men signing up for the recruiters' roles, Arlington Heights women started Red Cross Auxiliaries to create "comfort kits" each soldier received, containing toilet items needed in training camp. They also rolled strips of linen into bandages to be supplied to Red Cross units serving in France. The Food Administration Board handed out cards that went in people's front windows supporting the conservation of food and elimination of waste. Garden plots replaced lawns and filled vacant lots in the village. Sewing machines were installed in a room contributed by Mrs. E.N. Berbecker above the tailor shop at 7 Davis Street, and women turned out army clothing items by the boxful, including:

- 33 shoulder wraps
- 70 operating leggings
- 18 hospital shirts
- 110 towels

Arlington Heights, Illinois

- 7 pairs of socks
- 1 sweater
- 3 pairs of wristlets
- 3 scarves

The Library Committee of the Women's Club collected 100 books and hundreds of magazines for the training camps.[25]

Meatless days, wheatless days and heatless days were endured as a form of rationing on the homefront. In the training camps, an influenza epidemic—the Spanish flu—tore through the recruits, killing eleven at Camp Grant near Rockford, Illinois, where some of the Arlington Heights boys trained.

Many of those Arlington Heights soldiers who arrived in France were German farmers who spoke the language fluently. They were in immediate demand by military intelligence units for interrogation of prisoners and guarding captured Germans who did not realize German speakers were listening to conversations. In 1918, as the war came to an end, whole German units often surrendered to German-speaking American troops, saving a lot of young lives. Altogether, 133 Arlington Heights men took the train into Chicago to sign up to fight in the "War to End All Wars."

On November 7, 1918, Professor N. Moore Banta received a telephone call telling him that the war was over. With great excitement, he bounded from his house and, clutching an old bugle, leaped into his Ford flivver and sped off down Dunton Avenue blaring away on his horn and shouting to all that the war was over. The town blazed with excitement. Firecrackers were set off. Shotguns were fired in the air. Housewives beat on dishpans. Everyone had a great time. And four days later—after careful verification—they did it all over again when the war *actually* came to an end on November 11.

In August 1919, the boys were on their way home. Arlington Heights sprung for a huge welcome celebration. The *Cook County Herald* that month headlined the news: "Large Monument Purchased—Extensive Decorations—Big Eats Promised—Fun for All!"

A marble monument topped with a bronze eagle listing the names of the 133 men and boys who marched to war was erected in Memorial Park. On September 6, 1919, under brilliant sunshine, the village was a patriotic vision in red, white and blue bunting. American flags flew from every porch as the men of the 129th Infantry lined up rank on rank across South Vail Avenue. The village lined the curbs; pretty girls with flowers in their hats and rosettes pinned to their shirtwaists grinned and waved at the young men and fathers and brothers who stepped off in platoon formation of squads in line and crossed the railroad tracks by the old train station. The troops followed the Arlington Heights Marching Band under the baton of Army Lieutenant

Arlington Heights Marches Off to War

Rex Volz. The members of the largely German band put their backs into the music with Teutonic precision and residents cheered as 131 men who had gone to war came home.

The abbreviated parade marched to the school playground, where a farm-style picnic feast was laid out for everyone. Mayor Peter Mors gave a speech and the men's commanding officer in France arrived by train in time to add stories about their adventures "over there." Silver medals were struck for every returning soldier. Two gold medals were presented to the parents of two boys who did not come back, Theodore Heimsoth, who perished at sea, and David H. Hodges, who was killed in France.

The band kept the celebration lively with dance music to work off that trencherman's spread. When the festivities eventually ended, the soldiers adjourned by buggy, wagon and foot to the homes of families, to strolls with sweethearts and to the long bars at the Union, the American and the Wheeling House, where their money was worthless long after the gas lamps were lit.

Chapter 6

PROHIBITION—THE BEGINNING AND END IN 1919

Two society-changing events took place in the year following the Great War: prohibition of alcoholic beverages became a law via the Volstead Act, and Congress gave women the right to vote by passing the Nineteenth Amendment. Both of these traumatic measures had a great impact on Arlington Heights. They revealed a gritty side to the small farm town that many had taken for a pushover.

Prohibition of alcoholic beverages for sale or consumption came as a severe blow to most of the community. The Temperance movement had its roots deep among the Yankee settlers as far back as 1855. Numerous societies, such as the Women's Christian Temperance Union and the Anti-Saloon League, had campaigned for years. In 1910, a branch of the Illinois Anti-Saloon League was organized in Arlington Heights with the support of several churches. The "Drys" considered liquor the ruination of family life and the root of every sort of crime and bestiality. Considerable celebration greeted the Volstead Act among the Yankee churchgoers.

However, most people were motivated by nurture, not scripture, particularly the descendants of European settlers. Also, the soldiers who had gone to fight objected to the law that was passed when they had no vote while serving their country. A certain underground patriotic fervor to flout the new law gripped the population. People who had never tasted liquor were suddenly seeking out restaurants that served whiskey and gin in coffee cups. Recipes for various wines, including cherry, dandelion, currant and plum, were swapped like dress patterns. The law did permit the distilling of a small quantity of wine for family use only.

But as the '20s began to roar, the various criminal mobs that had carved up Chicago to squeeze money out of political corruption, gambling, prostitution and the protection racket turned avaricious eyes on supplying booze to the thirsty. It was a bonanza. Coincidentally, in 1919, Johnny "The Brain" Torrio imported an old pal from New York to help manage Big Jim Colosimo's whorehouses. The big kid with the scarred face was named Alphonse Capone and became Torrio's successor in time to expand the bootleg booze business into new territories. While most of Capone's turf wars involved the "Bugs" Moran and Dion O'Banion outfits on Chicago's North Side, he also rubbed hard against Roger Touhy, the beer baron of Des Plaines.

Since Des Plaines was only a few miles down the railroad tracks from Arlington Heights, visits were paid to local saloon and shop owners by large men driving big cars. They unloaded a full complement of slot machines and punch boards to decorate most village social establishments.

As gambling moved in, the Chicago illegal booze industry discovered enough people living in the countryside who were willing to greatly expand their little family winemaking into a considerable volume of harder stuff for distribution. Giant pot stills were built into innocent-looking homes that turned out gallons of busthead a day. Whole Arlington Heights neighborhoods smelled like cooking corn mash. Federal authorities were on the phone to Mayor Flentie to crack down. Flentie had no money to hire more police so he deputized the village board, which became a flying squad of shotgun-armed door-kickers, and out they went at night.

That none of these booze-sniffing vigilantes was killed or wounded was a miracle, but their work kept the feds happy. Following the stock market crash of 1929, Flentie advised the mob that he would not invite additional heat from Chicago law and the slot machines and punch boards could stay in place if Arlington Heights got a piece of the action. With that skim off the top, the village bought five hundred feet of fire hose, seats for the baseball diamond and a new Plymouth police squad car. There was a brief stir in the press following the revelation, but nothing ever came of it and soon all the gambling hardware was history.

The historical right to vote that was granted to women in 1919 played a major role in the education of village children for decades to come. Though the Nineteenth Amendment was passed in 1919, its ratification took place between 1914 and 1920, before the last of the states ratified the new law. That period of time was critical to Arlington Heights.

Beginning in 1907, the growing population and need for higher education for village children caused a number of problems. High school was considered to be the equivalent of a college education in rural communities at that time. Grades one through eight were considered sufficient. By 1914, high school classes were being taught in scattered classrooms wherever space could be

Prohibition—The Beginning and End in 1919

found. A vote was ordered to create a community high school district for areas including Arlington Heights, Wheeling, Elk Grove and part of Palatine. Of the 1,269 votes cast on the issue, the men's and women's votes had to be kept separate, because Illinois had not yet ratified the Nineteenth Amendment.

The legislators of the time, unfortunately, were in a complete muddle. They failed to validate the Nineteenth Amendment, so the women's votes were thrown out. The high school was out. Then, later, under pressure, the legislature validated women's suffrage. The women's votes counted and the school district was voted in by sixteen votes. But then, on a technicality, the legislature threw out Arlington Heights's school act and in doing so invalidated eighty other districts in Illinois. The school was out. Realizing its blunder, the legislature restored all the school districts *except* in Arlington Heights. There was still no school. Finally, in 1923, Arlington High School became a reality. But members of the graduating class of 1923 never attended the school—they just graduated from the building that was finally erected just east of the railroad tracks on Euclid Avenue.

While the village and the voters were hammering out the new high school district, other wheels were in motion that would put the final stamp on Arlington Heights's transportation core. In 1918, legislator and Arlington Heights board member Albert Volz was seated in a C&NW passenger coach musing as he peered out the window at the passing landscape. Automobiles were reaching out into what were being called "suburbs" of Chicago. Greater access to these farm communities meant growth. This growth meant more business opportunities, and Albert was a far-seeing entrepreneur. The only road access to Arlington Heights was from Rand Road by way of either Euclid Avenue or Foundry Street—both two-lane gravel affairs. Across from Volz sat his companion, Cook County commissioner William Busse, another name affixed to many projects in the area. Volz suggested that a road paralleling the railroad tracks, properly graded and tarred for the use of automobiles and truck traffic, would open up the northwest suburbs. Busse agreed, and in 1922, construction was begun on Route 14, called the Northwest Highway—four lanes wide and passing through town after town along the C&NW right of way.[26]

In addition to all the business the new road brought into Arlington Heights, its long, straight stretches became irresistible to automobilists in their fast Marmons, Stutz Bearcats and Stanley speeders to race the high-stepping ten-wheeler locomotives. Rushing down the tree-lined parkway, they blazed past the train station, the old freight shed and the siding where the farmers shipped their milk cans. They zoomed right into police Chief Skoog's motorcycle speed traps and got an expensive tour of the new village

Arlington Heights, Illinois

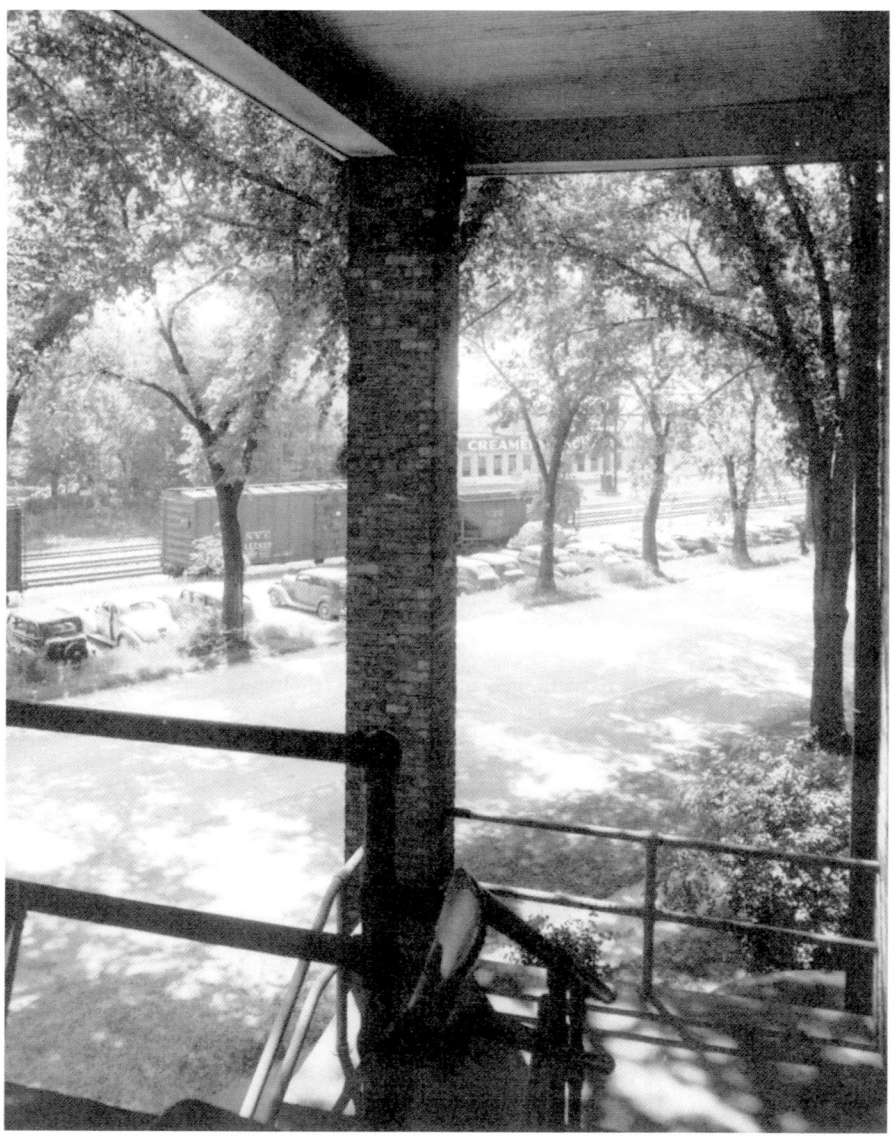

A view of Northwest Highway and railroad tracks as seen from the Altenheim Home. *Courtesy of Donna Turek.*

Prohibition—The Beginning and End in 1919

hall. Even years later, the broad, straight avenue had not lost its allure. In the 1930s, LeVern Gieseke got his thrills on Route 14:

"There was a cop called 'Killer' Carson. He'd chase us out of town. We'd drive down the gravel road by the race track at 100 miles an hour. Then we'd get to Palatine and he'd turn around. In those days they only followed you within their jurisdiction. But Chief Skoog, he picked us up off the ground, one hand each, and said, 'That's enough. Next time you're going to jail.'"[27]

Northwest Highway did not go unnoticed by another entrepreneur who had big plans. Curley Brown stood by the railroad tracks and looked far into the distance west along Wilke Road. He saw endless farmland and weed plots taking up the space meant for his racetrack. Brown was a horse racing millionaire with fifty years of experience; he had built tracks in Florida, Maryland, Havana and New Orleans. He had a gift for gab and knew what high-roller investors wanted to hear. No sooner had betting become legal in the state than he visualized a track near Chicago's action. Serviced by train—racetrack specials wedged into the C&NW's schedule—and now by the four-lane Northwest Highway, the Arlington Heights location was choice.

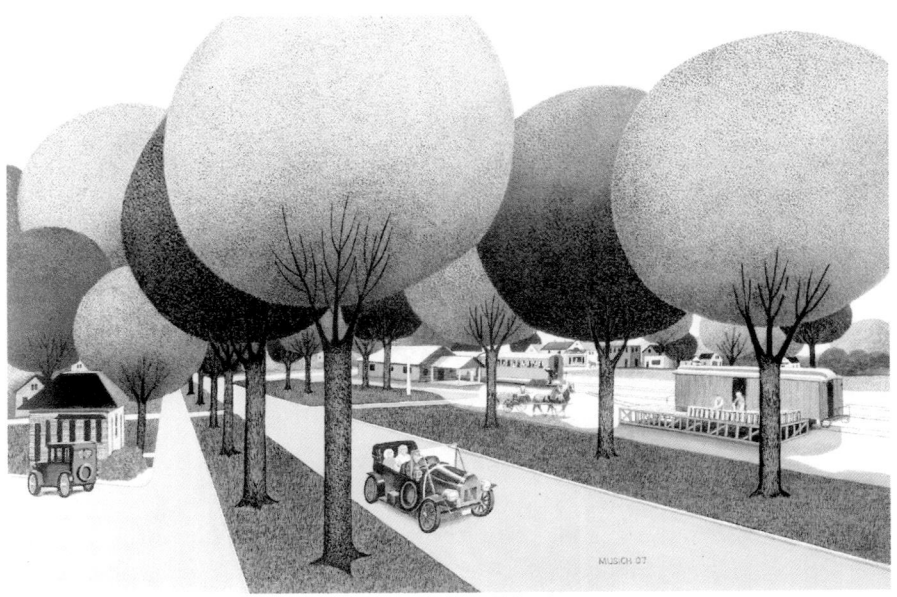

Drivers speed past the trains and siding where workers unload milk cans on the "milk switch" track in Arlington Heights. *Painting by Jack Musich.*

Arlington Heights, Illinois

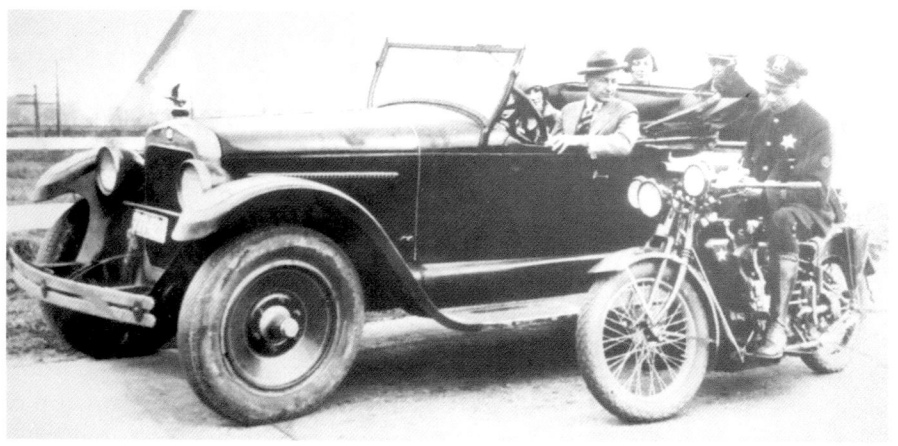

A policeman stopping a speeder on Northwest Highway, a favorite route for drag-racing enthusiasts. *Courtesy of the Arlington Heights Police Department.*

A plot of 1,200 acres of land was calculated for the track and parking. A collection of investors was corralled to the amount of $2 million and twelve farms were purchased, all through the offices of local broker Walter Krause. During the land purchases, Brown and the investors kept mum concerning the intended use of the land. As it was, the money men paid top dollar—between $1,100 and $1,700 an acre—to the farmers. The papers were signed on June 17, 1927.

Five hundred workers arrived—some with families—to a shack town that ran along Euclid Avenue. They set about building an eight-hundred-foot-long by ninety-five-foot-high grandstand with an attached clubhouse that accommodated eighteen thousand racing fans. Worked on seven days a week, the grandstand and clubhouse required 600,000 tons of steel and were finished in ten days, complete with red roof and bright green shutters. Klehm Nurseries contracted to provide three hundred apple trees to border the Euclid Avenue side of the track, obscuring the view for nonpaying customers.

As the edifice rose, Curley and his cohorts were dealing with Hawthorn and Washington Park racetracks to cede some days from their schedule. This battle eventually ended with Arlington Park getting an eighteen-day racing schedule. The track opened on October 13, 1927. The C&NW, nicknamed the "Cheap and Nothing Wasted," had uncharacteristically provided three sidings off its main line for special race trains. Long limousines arrived bearing VIPs, including Charles G. Dawes—the vice president of the United States—and wealthy industrialists, local and national politicians.

Prohibition—The Beginning and End in 1919

Memberships to the American National Jockey Club could be purchased for $10,000 by only a select group of supporting angels. In addition, the racetrack was the United States' only double track—a turf track within the dirt track—and was operated in partnership with both Belmont and Saratoga Racing organizations.

The opening day festivities included shiny-suit horseplayers with their tootsies on their arms who strolled next to raccoon-coated dapper lads boldly swigging from silver flasks. It was a chill, blustery day, and $3,000 had been spent on cinders for ground cover just to keep the mud off gentlemen's spats. The opening race was won by the favorite, Luxembourg, with Joe Bollero aboard.

In addition to putting Arlington Heights on the international map as breeders from foreign countries brought their horses to race, the track also introduced a whole new culture to the village. Track workers followed the racing season from state to state like gypsies. They moved into on-track

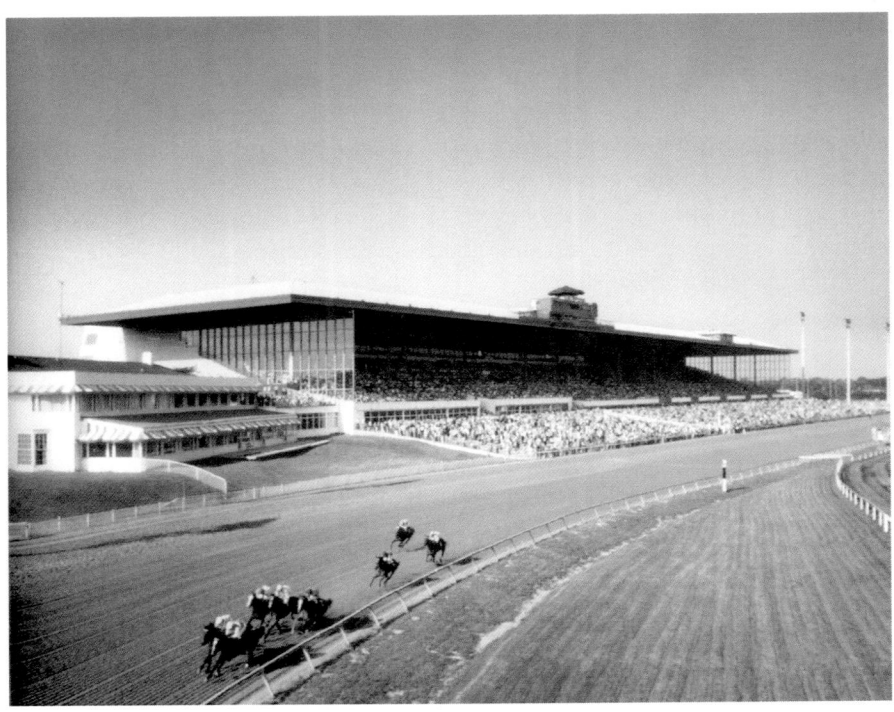

And they're off! Arlington Park Racecourse, built in the late 1920s. *Courtesy of the Arlington Park Racecourse.*

housing with their families, used the village facilities and moved away at the end of the season. Horse owners and trainers either stayed in hotels or became the guests of local residents who set aside rooms and served meals. Kids in school found jobs as "hot walkers," leading the horses in long walks to cool down after training workouts. Local charities benefited from Arlington Park when charity races were held, and a portion of the winnings that day went to support a number of deserving causes.

And, of course, the more things change, the more they stay the same. Curley Brown was given the bum's rush out of town when the track's first year ended up $100,000 in the red—especially when it was discovered that Curley had lined his pockets with $283,000 profit from the land leases, $61,000 on construction costs and $60,000 from wagers. State control of racing in the '20s was much more casual than today. By 1928, Brown's health had broken and he was ripe for picking by the Chicago mob. To protect their investment, the industrialists and high rollers who had backed the track raised $2 million in twenty minutes to buy out his share and see him on his way. The mob was shut out and took considerable umbrage.

Two gentlemen beer barons, Terry Druggan and Frankie Lake, took it upon themselves to force their way into the deal. First, they tried to get Curley shipped off to a sanitarium. When that ploy failed, at 3:10 a.m. on the day the papers were signed, a long black limousine pulled up at the Arlington Park entrance. Out of the car trooped men with guns, bolt cutters and cans of gasoline to break in and burn the place down. When the locks proved intractable, a fusillade of gunfire ripped through the night as the gunmen sought to blast the locks with .45-caliber slugs. From inside, night guards fired at the intruders. Gunfire, lead clanging off iron bars, shouts and the curious peering out windows proved too much, and the gunmen fled.[28]

Another part of that new culture was the flip side of the infusion of money into Arlington Heights's coffers from taxes, merchandise and service purchases and utilities use. Residents came face to face with big-city problems they had never known before. Dr. Robert Muench, one of the handful of practicing GPs in town, recalls, "A track worker collapsed on the street in town. I was called and he begged me to give him 'a shot' and 'everything would be okay.' I suggested he go to the hospital and he got up and walked away."

On another occasion, "a well known jockey came to my office to offer a 'sure thing'—meaning a fixed race—if I would go with him and place the bets. I told him I 'didn't bet on horses.'"

Neither did the track advance the cause of Prohibition. Ranging down Euclid Street was a shanty town erected for the Slavic and Irish construction

Prohibition—The Beginning and End in 1919

workers. After a long day wielding a hammer or shouldering a hod of brick, the men went home to a hefty dram of pacheen—a clear alcoholic spirit made of potatoes—or a flowery jolt of plum slivovitz distilled from the fruit of Arlington's plentiful orchards. A haze of cooking booze hung over the area and the police made frequent visits.

But if there were problems, Arlington Park frequently came to the village's aid. During the Great Depression of the 1930s, jobs were scarce, as was folding money. The track provided both to residents with such labor-intensive jobs as covering the track with straw for the winter and hooking hay bales off the trucks. Seasonal cash paid for rented housing and services. Its reputation also gave status to the community that helped lure manufacturing, and the track's tax contribution helped keep the village infrastructure operating. Over the years, Arlington Park became a good neighbor and a working partner with the town.

Chapter 7

PULLING TOGETHER THROUGH THE GREAT DEPRESSION

An overhead view of Arlington Heights in 1929 shows a prosperous farm community. From a pokey little wide space on either side of a single railroad track, the rails had expanded to two main line tracks and two long sidings that serviced coal silos, sugar beet silos, oil storage tanks, a rolling mill and lumber yard. Three banks and a loan company were busy institutions. Shops, auto garages and sales showrooms stood near hardware stores, bakeries, barbershops and saloons that also served meals. While farms pressed in close to the village boundaries, more and more residents commuted to and from jobs in Chicago and lived in Arlington Heights's single-family homes on the expanding grid of side streets.

"Buy now and pay later" credit plans had allowed Arlington Heights residents to afford many of the luxuries that electricity brought into their homes: radios, vacuum cleaners and washing and sewing machines. Electric lights blazed on the streets. Families made trips to exotic Sarasota, Florida, or the Carolina beaches, or even New York City. Many people put their saved money to work in the New York Stock Exchange, and keeping track of Wall Street machinations became a popular pastime for everyone from taxi drivers waiting for fares at the railroad station to farmers with some egg money put by.

The Roaring Twenties ended with a bang that year for many Americans. In October 1929 the stock market, teetering on a house of cards built on bad credit and bad loans, collapsed. The implosion that rocked major financial centers was barely felt in Arlington Heights. The November and December newspapers of that year hardly mention anything but financial pundits muttering about "corrections" and "confidence in our institutions." The ripple effect didn't reach the village until the following year.

Typically, farmers borrowed from the bank against the yield of next year's crop in order to buy seed, fertilizer and whatever else was needed

Arlington Heights, Illinois

for planting. The banks found themselves short of cash as people began defaulting on loan payments in order to meet their stock investment obligations. Companies suffered the same credit crunch and cut loose workers. Job losses forced some residents to default on their 1928–29 taxes, and that lack of income forced Arlington Heights to hunt for service cuts. One of these involved the school districts.

Teachers' salaries suffered severe cutbacks to the point that they were paid with "warrants"—pieces of paper worth ten and fifteen dollars—presented to shopkeepers and other providers in lieu of cash that could be turned in for dollars as the tax money became available. Eventually, as the tax money remained a trickle, city employees at all levels were paid with vouchers and anticipation warrants. Few businesses could afford to accept the warrants at face value. Even Chief Skoog and the police force had to accept pay cuts.

In the Great Plains states, wheat and corn had been overplanted and crop yields sat in silos as prices plummeted. This financial crisis was followed by a severe drought, and the prairie winds blew hot and heavy across topsoil that had no grass roots to hold it in place. Huge dust storms gathered the soil in dark clouds that scoured the country from west to east, rolling over Chicago and Arlington Heights heading all the way to New York.

Since it was still a farm community, the village was insulated from some of the worst ravages of the Great Depression that lasted from 1930 to 1941. Vegetables, tomatoes, fruit orchards and cornfields abounded, and a system of barter was established. A bag of corn bought a haircut. Dr. Robert Muench remembers taking home baskets of vegetables for house calls as late as postwar 1947. Some homemakers raised chickens for eggs and meat. Rabbit became a popular entrée in many homes. Hunting season was largely ignored and bringing down pheasants on the wing became a serious survival business.

Dolores Bokelman remembers that her dad couldn't work, so he raised chickens in their basement.

> *He and my mom had a little delivery route and they'd go into Norwood Park and Edison Park and deliver their fresh-drawn chickens and the eggs they'd picked up on Friday night and my grandmother would stay with us while they made their deliveries. That's how they made some money during the Depression to survive. Later his brother had a farm out on Palatine road and he allowed my dad to build a shed there where he could raise his chickens. We didn't know any different. We had two dresses—one you wore one week while the other was being washed and on Sunday you put the clean*

Pulling Together through the Great Depression

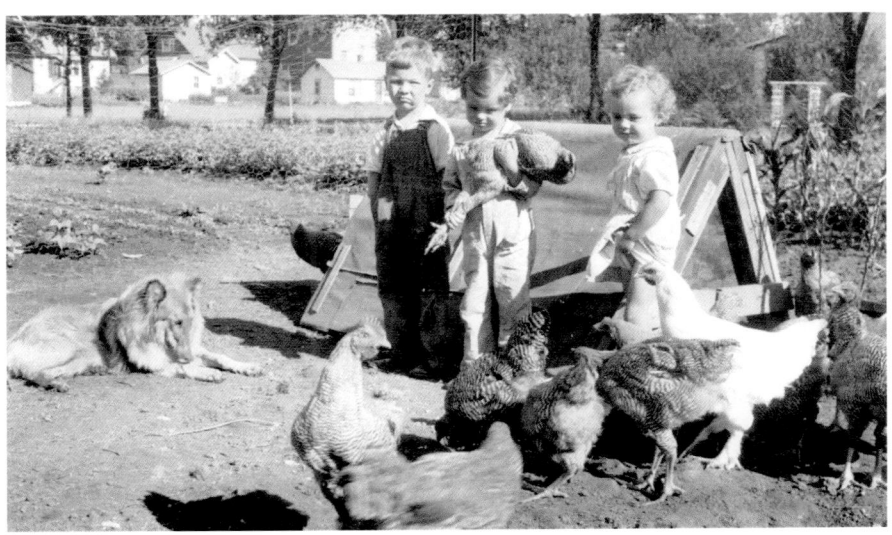

Many families raised chickens during the Depression. This picture was taken on the east side of north Pine Street, a block south of St. James Church. *From left*: Robert, Catherine and Dorothy Thiel. *Courtesy of Catherine Quigg.*

one on when you went to church and then you wore that one for the rest of the week.[29]

Shirley Brown grew up during the Great Depression, and she remembers:

I had my father's time books—he was a carpenter and one year he made $1200. He took any kind of work he could do. He fixed the minister's car for 50 cents. You took your money where you could get it. A quart of milk was 3 cents. My grandfather lived on North Evergreen Avenue. It was wonderful. They had a big garden where they grew grapes, apples and vegetables and they had chickens.

I remember we would put cardboard in our shoes. We would lay them down, draw around the shape of the shoes and cut the cardboard to fit.[30]

Anthony Dattilo was typical of the small-business owners who made up downtown Arlington Heights. He moved to the village in 1932 and opened a fruit and vegetable market on West Campbell Street next to the Cake Box Bakery. Running his business cost him ten dollars a year for a license, and he lived at 1423 North Belmont with his wife Hilda and their four children. His house stood on a five-acre lot. They had a garden and kept a horse, turkeys,

Arlington Heights, Illinois

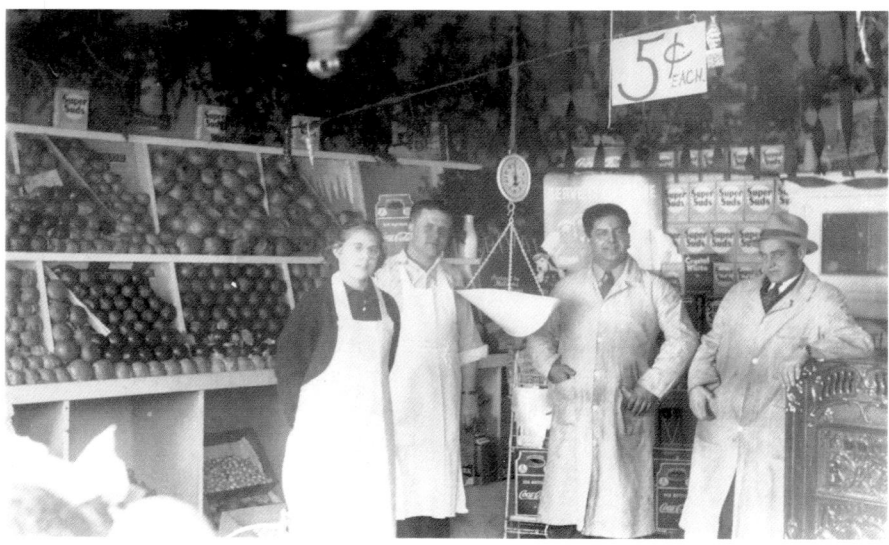

Inside Dattilo's produce and grocery store, 1930s. Anthony Dattilo is second from right; Art Schaefer is on the far right. The other two are unknown. *Courtesy of Don Dattilo.*

A business license granted to Anton Dattilo on August 10, 1936, to operate a fruit and vegetable store on Campbell Street between Evergreen and Vail. The cost was five dollars and the license was good for six months. His name should read "Anthony," not "Anton." *Courtesy of Don Dattilo.*

Pulling Together through the Great Depression

chickens and pigs. Following the tradition of small markets in those days, he also had an open truck that he drove around town. Its roof was canvas supported by posts with leather straps hanging down on the sides, where he hung bunches of bananas. He would park and then walk the block calling out, "I have potatoes for five cents!" As he walked, shouting out his specials, housewives came from their homes with their purses and bought from the back of the truck.[31]

For Arlington Heights residents who were suddenly out of work, any kind of income was welcome. They came to the village hall looking for menial labor jobs. It didn't matter if they had once worked as a bank teller or a clerk accountant; they would sweep floors or wield a shovel to feed their families. The village had little to offer, but it set up a Relief Committee composed of one member from each church and the community nurse. This group helped scrounge up bags of groceries and clothing for the needy as well as offering job guidance.

Both the Arlington Heights State Bank and the People's Bank closed. The only source of cash in the village was the real estate loan office of Krause and Kehe until the Arlington Heights National Bank opened in 1937.

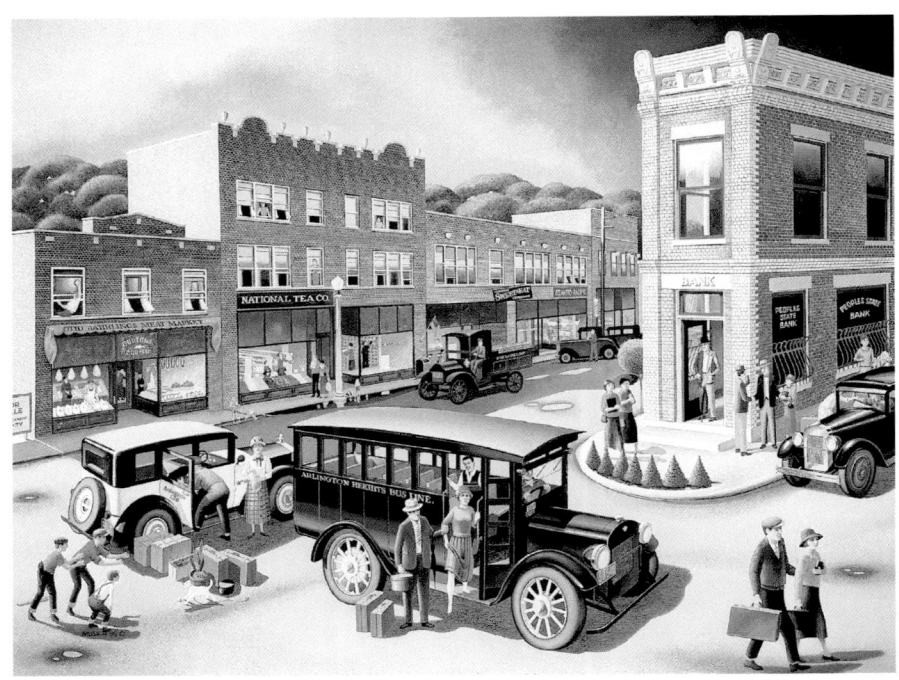

A taxi in front of People's Bank at the intersection of Campbell, Davis and Evergreen, 1920s. *Painting by Jack Musich.*

Arlington Heights, Illinois

By 1933, President Franklin Roosevelt had pushed through the National Recovery Act (NRA) and Mayor Julius Flentie—the same mayor who had skimmed money from the mob's slot machine take to improve village services—proposed a $50,000 waterworks improvement project to the trustees. He gathered further local support for the project—the village had needed it for years—and made a presentation to the Chicago Committee of the NRA. Everyone held their breath. Not only was the project approved, but the federal government ponied up $12,500, with the rest being paid off over the next twenty years at 4 percent interest. Flentie immediately began contracting to local labor and suppliers.

From this success, the village board stormed ahead to secure more jobs for the local economy. A regular village beautification plan had buildings painted, an old sewer torn up, landscaping planted and open ditches filled, much of which was paid for by a government Civic Works Grant of $15,000. Flentie waded through Roosevelt's New Deal in hip boots, plucking out a WPA grant here, a Civilian Conservation Corps project there, always pouring money and jobs back into the struggling community. In 1934, as unemployment rates peaked and four years of making ends meet had worn down most residents, someone at a board meeting suggested that a municipal swimming pool might be a good idea.

A year passed and the time came due for presentation of the Arlington Heights pool project to the government Works Project Administration. The land had been donated by Walter Krause, but for one reason or another no formal plan had survived over the months of debate. On the last day before the proposal was to be presented, Arlington's representatives showed up with a verbal pitch and not a scrap of supporting paper or blueprints. The WPA board in Niles, Illinois, threw up its hands in frustration. At that moment, Arlington Heights trustee Schneberger remembered that Glenview had had a public pool plan approved by this WPA body. He stepped forward and said, in effect, "We will use the Glenview plan as the model for our municipal pool."

The WPA board conferred and replied, in effect, "Oh, okay."

The *Daily Herald* newspaper proclaimed, "The dream of every kid in Arlington Heights and a great many of their elders, a swimming pool may be realized at practically no expense to the tax payers."

The village did have to come up with $15,000, but the bulk of the money, some $90,000, came from the WPA. Recreation Park became a village icon with its main building, adjoining pool and baseball field. Bob Frisk, a former sportswriter for the *Daily Herald*, remembered the field as it was in the mid-1940s:

Pulling Together through the Great Depression

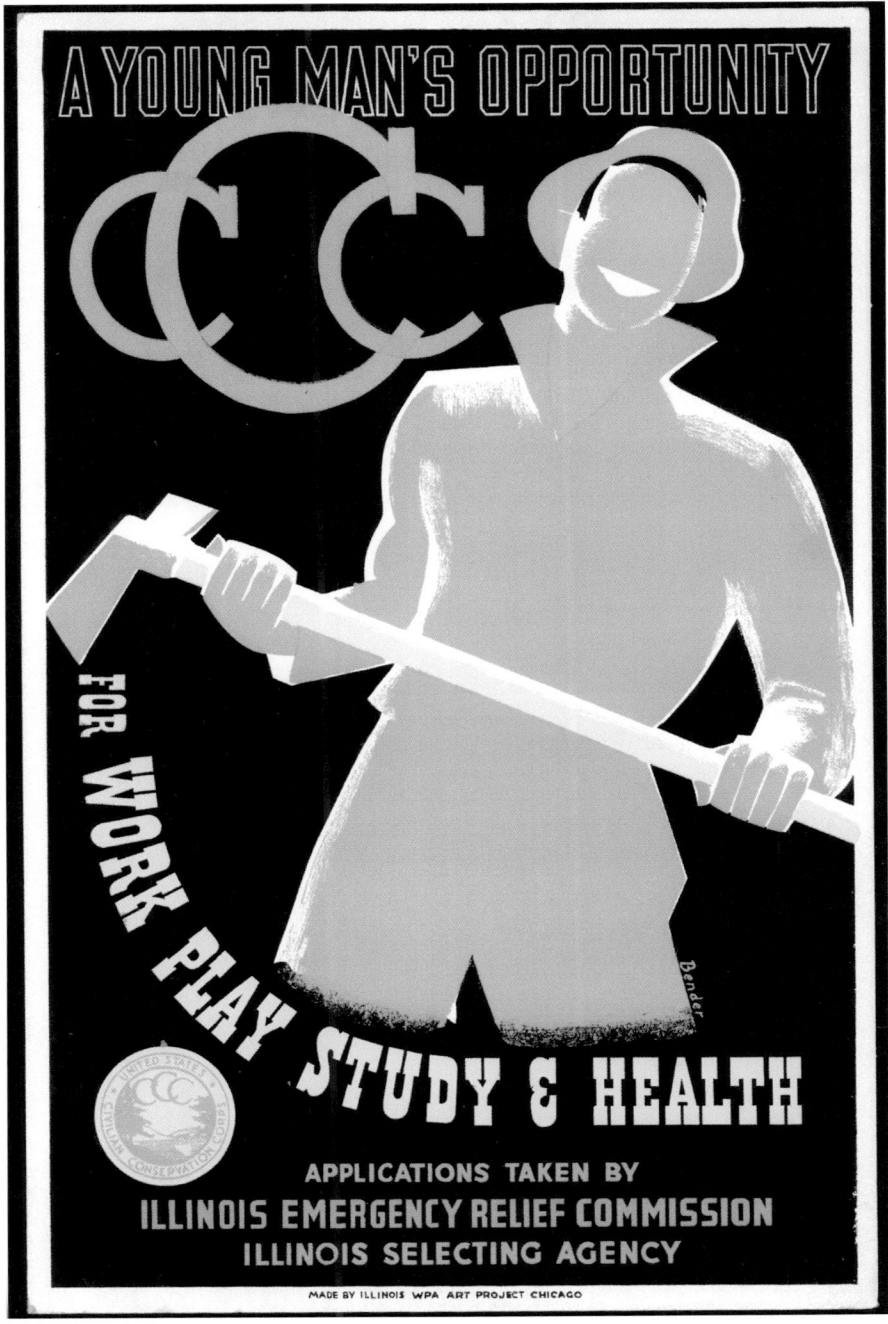

Civilian Conservation Corps poster. The CCC was part of President Roosevelt's plan to create jobs for young men. The CCC and the Works Progress Administration (WPA) helped build Recreation Park. *Courtesy of the Library of Congress.*

Arlington Heights, Illinois

I always went to Rec Park. Before television baseball came in they had a team called the Arlington Redwings, on which Lloyd Meyer played. We would go down to the park and watch them play double headers every Sunday. The whole town would show up. They were semi-pro teams. The guys were in their 30s and 40s. Lloyd was in college. One guy used to pitch for the Cardinals—Dick Bokelman. When I was small, I lived on South Belmont. At Park Street and State Road there was a field where we'd play all the time. There was no organized Little League. Nothing organized, that's the big difference. We just went out and played. Then it slowly started to change. Later, I announced Little League games. I don't know how I got the job. I would do two or three games a day. I was 13 or 14. I got paid $5 a game. My parents in Scarsdale could hear me announce the games from Rec Park.

It was a picnic atmosphere; they had a big grandstand. It was at what they call Lloyd Meyer field now. In high school, they had a youth center that they called the Ramble Inn at Rec Park. You went there on Wednesday and Friday nights. They had TV down there—and dancing. The girls would dance with the girls and the guys sat around and watched boxing.[32]

Lloyd Meyer remembers his days with the Redwings:

I played with the Redwings right out of high school. They were all older; in their 30s. I happened to step into the situation—they needed a guy and I

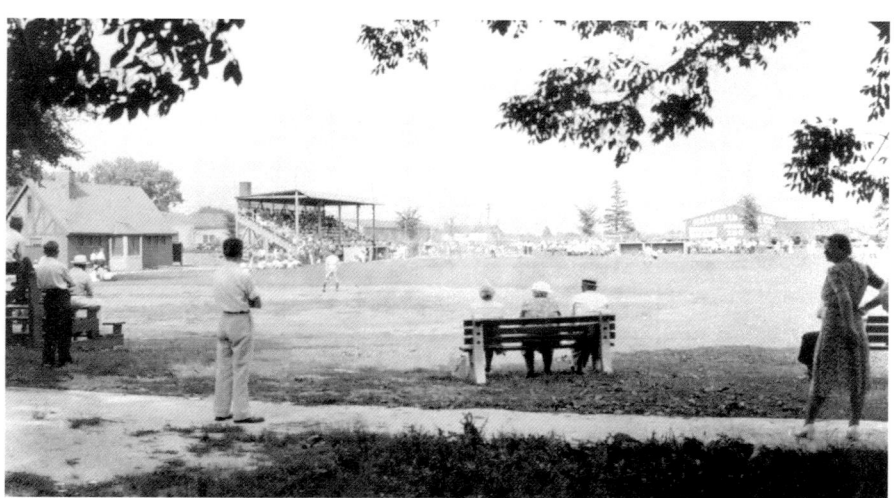

Baseball field, Recreation Park, 1940s. The Arlington Redwings, a minor league team, played here on Sundays up to the early 1950s. *Courtesy of Lloyd Meyer.*

Pulling Together through the Great Depression

played well. I played some semi-pro ball before TV came along. Before TV we used to fill that grandstand when we played on Sundays and holidays. I was in seventh heaven. Fans wore Redwing red hats and walked around with handfuls of red ticket stubs. To sit in the grandstand you had to pay a dollar and the red stub showed you'd paid.

Lloyd coached an American Legion–sponsored team after high school and the team went to the national finals. When he wasn't coaching, he worked for his father's dairy, which had deep roots in the community.

In 1956 they had just started building the town of Rolling Meadows. And I remember trying to get customers in Hasbrook. We had almost a whole route out there. That was the new business we picked up in 1956–1960. There was all home delivery then. At one time I counted about 17 dairies. We went out and just looked for business. It was cutthroat. At one point we had seven trucks that went out every day—three days a week each had about 125–150 stops. When we lost business because of the stores carrying milk, we started vending and have been vending ever since. Now I service ten schools and about ten restaurants.

Our dairy is behind the house at 1003 Euclid. That whole triangle was Fesler Dairy and farm. He had that yellow house and a farm in the back. There was a chicken coop where that apartment house is today.

When the war came, I can remember putting ration stamps in the books and sending them to the government. People paid with stamps, for the butter, for example and we'd put them in the book, send it to the government and they'd send us the money.

Throughout the Great Depression, Mayor Julius Flentie and the village board tirelessly pursued every government dollar and turned those dollars into jobs and a better standard of life. The new Arlington Heights theatre that opened in 1929 ("Arlington Heights has talking pictures!" reported the *Daily Herald*) was kept supplied with two-reelers and shorts that took residents' minds off financial troubles. In Chicago, the 1933 Century of Progress Fair opened and continued into 1934, only a train ride away to the fantasy of tomorrow created on the lakefront. Visitors could see the world record–breaking Burlington Zephyr streamlined train, climb aboard the Rocket Ride, experience the visions of the future—or just enjoy the nude feather-fan dance of Sally Rand.

By the end of the 1930s, the world once more intruded on Arlington Heights's bucolic isolation. Outside speakers for a variety of causes were often guests at the various churches. The large German population drew more than its share of interest from the American-Nazi Bund and its related organizations. In 1937, the Lutheran Laymen's Club hosted the Reverend H. Blanke, who described what he termed "the truth about Germany" to counteract the "malicious propaganda" circulated by jealous enemies of the Third Reich. He praised Adolf Hitler's policies toward the Jews and German militarism. The following year, Dr. Albert Wild of the University of Berlin lectured the Methodist Men's Club. He supported Hitler's economic program and efforts to "bring about a healthful German race."

Arlington Heights residents quickly had their curiosity assuaged and, in letters to the editor of the *Daily Herald*, stated their disapproval of the "tyrannical and evil" regime that had occupied Germany. From 1938 to 1940, newspapers, magazines, radio broadcasts and film newsreels were saturated with opposing isolationist and interventionist viewpoints. Conversations turned away from the tribulations of the Great Depression toward the more global concerns of yet another war with Germany. Young men began joining the reserves so they could select their branch of the armed forces should war come. Ten years of the Depression had hardened and toughened American youth. Those years had laid the foundation for the army and navy that were eventually called into action following the Japanese attack on Pearl Harbor on December 7, 1941.

Once again, the young men and women of Arlington Heights went into uniform to fight a war on two fronts against implacable enemies. And, once again, residents of the village along the railroad track did their part.

Chapter 8

ARLINGTON HEIGHTS ON THE HOMEFRONT

Village participation in World War II was far more personal than in the Great War of 1914–18. We had been attacked and more than one thousand Americans had been killed. To Europe, writhing under the onslaught of Hitler's military, the Japanese air raid on Pearl Harbor was a godsend. When Hitler joined Japan in declaring war on the United States, the deal was sealed. The Great Depression–crippled machine that had been the American economy began to repair itself as lights went on in silent factories around the country. The call went out for war production, for rationing of essential materials and for civilians, male and female, to report for duty.

One of the largest war industries northwest of Chicago that attracted a considerable number of Arlington Heights residents was the Douglas Aircraft Company's huge plant at Mannheim Road, Higgins Road and Devon Avenue, where the company built the two- and four-engine Douglas C-47 and C-54 Skytrain transport aircraft. The factory was located at Orchard Place Airport/Douglas Field, a sprawling piece of land that was eventually renamed after a World War II flying hero, Lieutenant Commander Edward "Butch" O'Hare. He became America's first combat ace in 1942 with five enemy planes shot down in one day. Even today, O'Hare Field's airport code is ORD, after its Orchard Field–Douglas Field original name.

After the grim realities of Depression-era employment, the war industries such as Douglas offered incentives to job seekers: "And you enjoy many special advantages…recreational opportunities such as dances, entertainment, sports, clubs and parties. Food in the plant restaurant is excellent and inexpensive. Money saving group insurance is available. And there is a Share-the-Ride program…It's easy to apply for a well-paid job at Douglas."[33]

Virtually everyone in Arlington Heights became caught up in the war on some level. The National Aeronautics Council printed up an *Aircraft Spotters*

Arlington Heights, Illinois

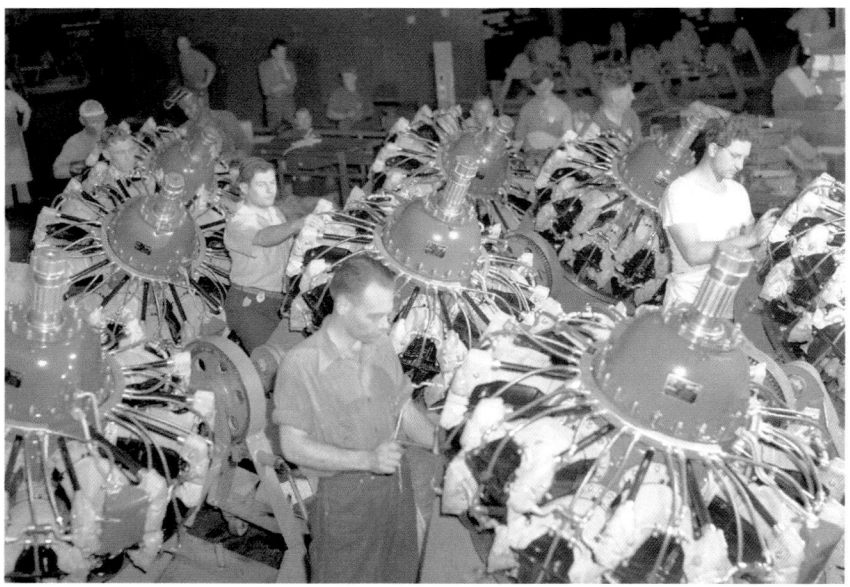

Factory workers in 1940s at a Douglas airplane assembly plant near Orchard Field (O'Hare Field today), building rotary engines. Many Arlington Heights residents worked there. *Courtesy of the Library of Congress.*

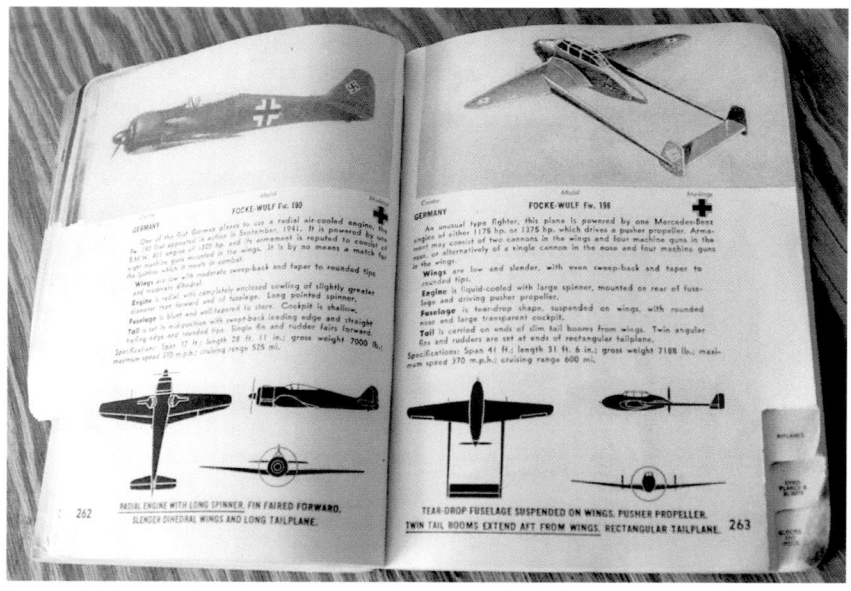

Airplane Spotters Handbook, used by civilians and air raid wardens during World War II. *Photo by Gerry Souter.*

Arlington Heights on the Homefront

Handbook in 1943. Chicago's importance as a rail hub, a port and a steel producer made it a potential target for enemy bombers. Learning to spot the various types of German and Japanese planes became a goal to more than one million plane spotters across the country. Kids in high school built recognition models while Boy Scout troops held contests using flash cards showing airplane silhouettes. The fact that none of the Axis powers had a long-range bomber that could reach Chicago seemed irrelevant. After all, London was being destroyed by fleets of bombers and the Japanese had managed a sneak attack on Pearl Harbor.

Arlington Heights homefront preparedness extended to creating a semiformal Home Guard. Shotguns and deer rifles came out of closets and an emergency rifle squad was formed from those too old or too young to serve in uniform. Their job was to be ready to assemble at a moment's notice should enemy parachutists descend into village cornfields.

In case some enemy bombs fell wide of their Chicago targets and came whistling down into Arlington Heights, the village created a demolition squad in 1942. Frank Sachs—probably the bravest man in town—volunteered to teach eager residents how to use dynamite to clear paths through bomb rubble for emergency vehicles. In case those errant bombs knocked out communications, the Boy Scouts and Cub Scouts trained for service as bicycle messengers, weaving their way through the devastation to spread the word.

Residents suddenly had more to worry about than crab grass with the possibility of incendiary bombs raining down on their neighborhoods. Manuals were distributed to demonstrate how to dispose of those nasty firebombs. Everyone was encouraged to clean out their attics of all flammable materials. Next, garden hoses must always be ready for use—but never, never, never spray water directly on a bomb, or the phosphorous would flare up and reduce the house to ash. The final tool required was a long-handled shovel. With this tool, the homeowner was supposed to pick up the fizzing bomb and dump it out the window, where it could be extinguished with a bucket of sand.

But the best protection was darkness. The enemy bombers could not hit what they could not see. Blackout drills were held in the neighborhoods and monitored by Civil Defense wardens. No slivers of light were permitted to show around blackout curtains.

Carl Weinrich was a warden during these drills and remembered people calling to him from behind their closed doors, "This is ridiculous. Do you really expect that some day we'll be bombed?"

All he could answer was, "Better to be prepared."[34]

Even smokers complied by cupping their cigarettes at night and smoking their pipes with the bowl pointed down so no enemy bombardier flying at

Arlington Heights, Illinois

thirty thousand feet could see that glowing tobacco coal and come down for a closer look.

While these preparations may seem fanciful, they were manifestations of people who wanted to do their part in the war effort—and at least they were voluntary. Many wartime rules and regulations clamped down hard on the civilian population. A curious dichotomy occurred as employment ramped up in factories and residents began earning paychecks again. Suddenly, as the needs of our soldiers overseas increased, daily life at home was curtailed.

Life wasn't all struggle and strife, or fear of enemy bombs. Kids of the 1940s and '50s figured out ways to have fun. In the winter, streets iced up and most people kept their cars in the garage because of gas and tire rationing. Jodee Gieseke remembers: "We used to ice skate on Evergreen Avenue—there wasn't much traffic, so we'd go ice skating right on the road instead of going all the way over to Recreation Park. Nobody was out."

Driving into Chicago or visiting friends and relatives in nearby towns was severely limited by gas rationing. Virtually half the drivers in the country and most in Arlington Heights had an "A" window sticker, which allowed

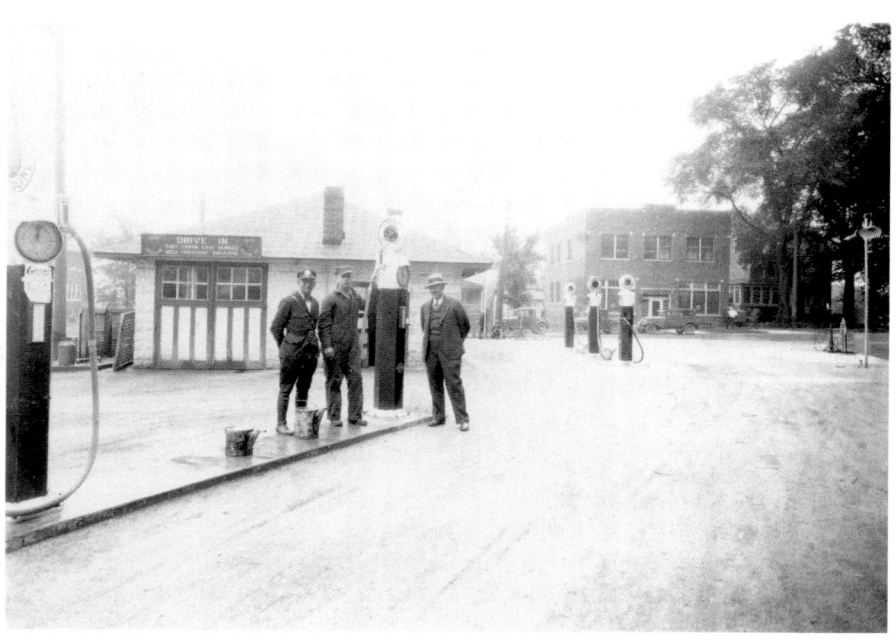

The Sterling Oil station on the northwest corner of Arlington Heights Road and Northwest Highway. *From left*: Officer Lester Dobbins, Don Gieseke and Gary Ackerman. *Courtesy of Donna Turek.*

Arlington Heights on the Homefront

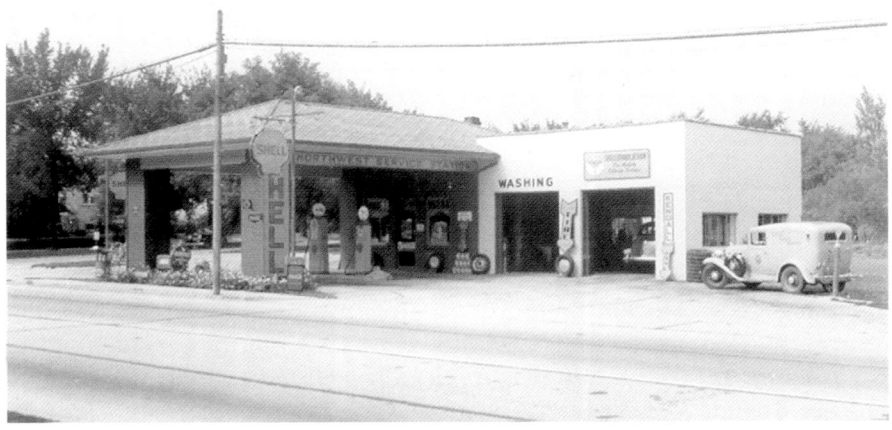

Horath Shell station, Northwest Highway and Belmont Avenue, 1930s. It is now Grandt's station. *Helen Horath estate.*

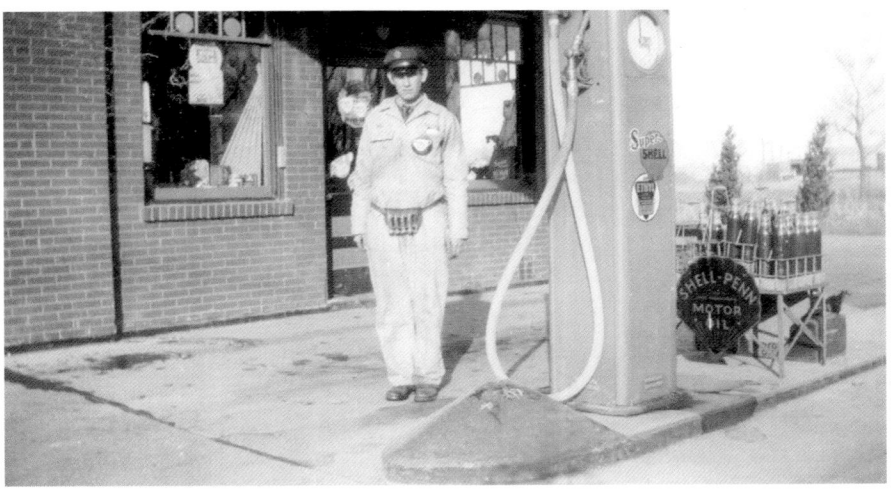

Virgil Horath in front of his Shell station, 1935. *Helen Horath estate.*

the gas station attendant to fill the tank with only two or four gallons of gas per week. She—yes, many attendants were female because the men were overseas—kept track of the weekly coupon use to avoid hoarding. The green "B" sticker was for driving deemed essential to the war effort: industrial war workers, for example, could purchase eight gallons a week. Red "C" stickers indicated physicians, ministers, mail carriers and railroad workers. "T," for truckers supplying the population with goods, received unlimited gallons of fuel.[35]

Rubber was another strategic commodity, since the Japanese had overrun Pacific rubber suppliers. Spare tires were impossible to find and scrap rubber was melted down and reapplied to old tires called "retreads." Many drivers simply stored their car for the duration and took the bus or train.

Even then, local train traffic was limited by national military priorities. Flatcars carrying trucks and tanks rumbled through downtown followed by troop trains painted olive drab. American flags flew everywhere. Arlington Heights as a town continued much as it had in Depression times before the war, still living within food and transportation restrictions, but now the young men and women were once again leaving for war. In 1942, the population who signed up for ration books numbered about 4,000. Of that number, 437 men, 16 women, 1 chaplain and 3 doctors left the village for war service. During that year, 75 men a week showed up at the Selective Service Board for screening. Not all of them passed.[36]

Men who couldn't fight with a rifle did so with a wrench or a jackhammer, or by patrolling streets at night to make sure that the blackout was complete. Women worked in war plants, planted victory gardens, formed canning clubs (putting up fruits and vegetables so nothing was wasted), rolled surgical bandages and collected old but clean clothes to be sent overseas in the "Bundles for Britain" campaign. Games and books were collected for American United Service Organization (USO) units, where soldiers spent off-duty hours. Kids roamed the streets with their wagons collecting tin pots, old buckets and even some of their toys for the scrap metal drives. Bundles of old newspapers were tossed up into trucks to be recycled. Local industries shifted their product lines to accept military contracts. Arlington Seating, a company that built school desks, began turning out wood crates for shipping torpedoes. Everywhere, posters exhorted civilians to avoid waste, conserve water, buy war bonds and take cooking grease to the butcher shop for recycling.

As Japanese Admiral Yamamoto exclaimed when he discovered that Pearl Harbor had been bombed before delivery of a formal declaration of war, "We have awakened a sleeping giant."

Arlington Heights on the Homefront

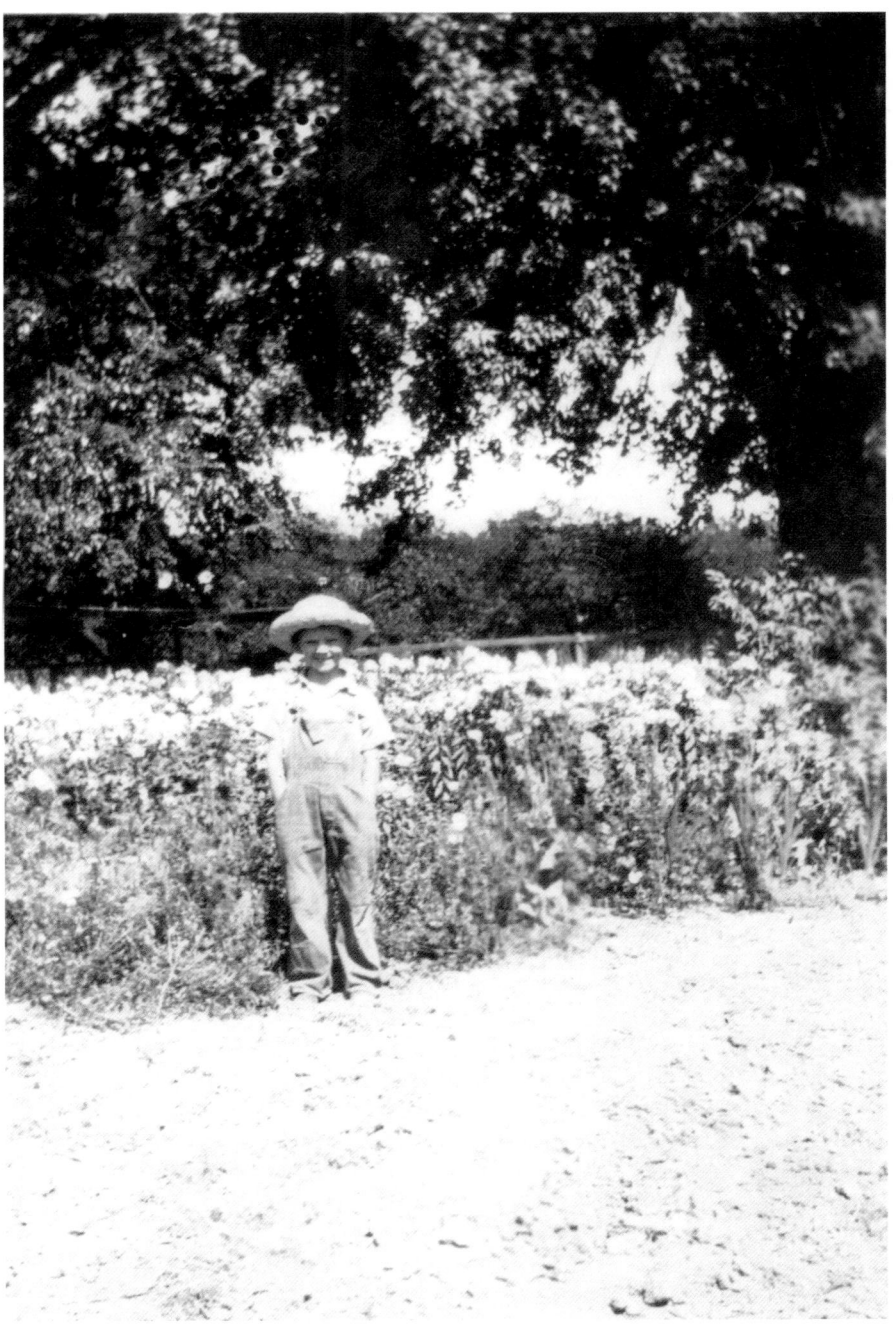

This and next page: First Lieutenant Wilbert Gieseke, USMCR. Here, as a child, circa 1930s. He was reported missing at sea on March 8, 1945. His body was never recovered. *Courtesy of Donna Turek.*

Arlington Heights, Illinois

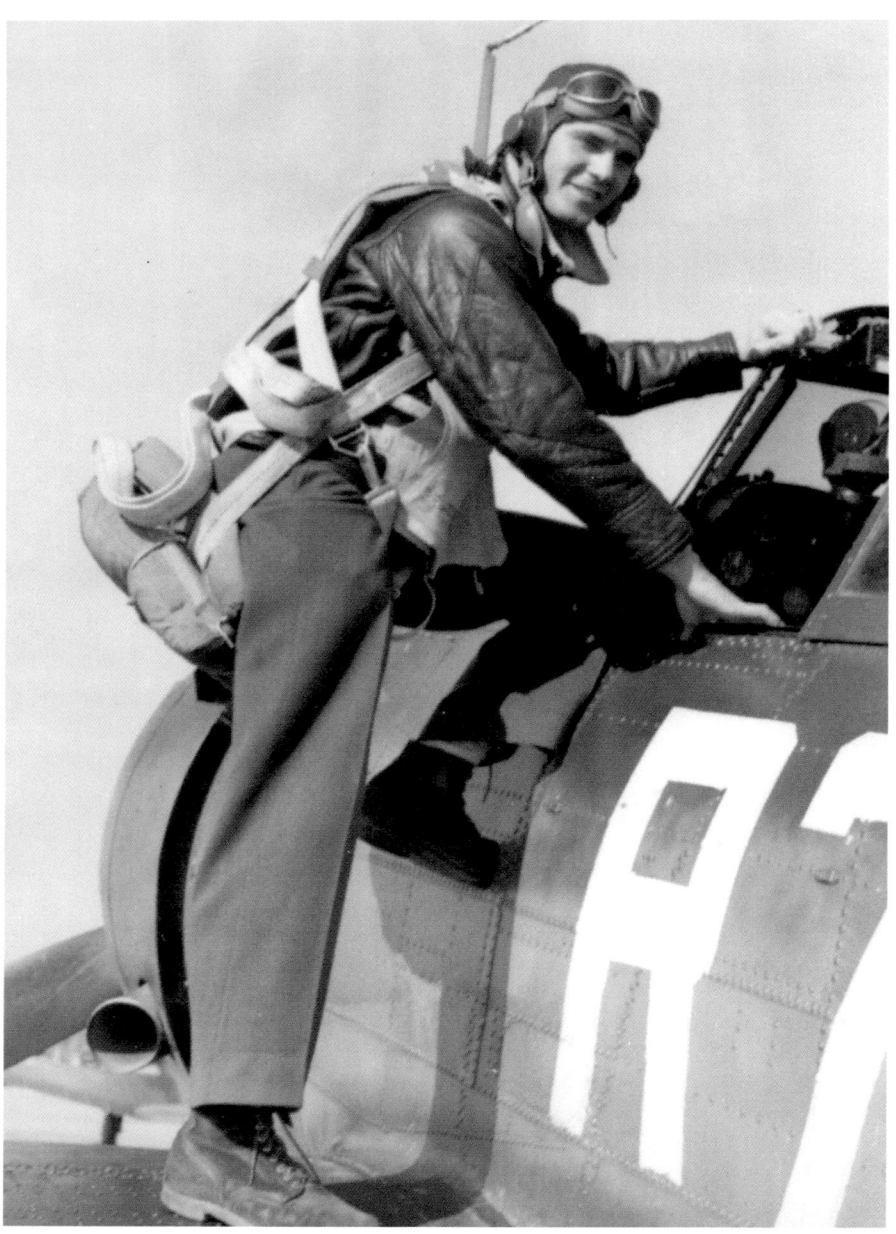

Arlington Heights on the Homefront

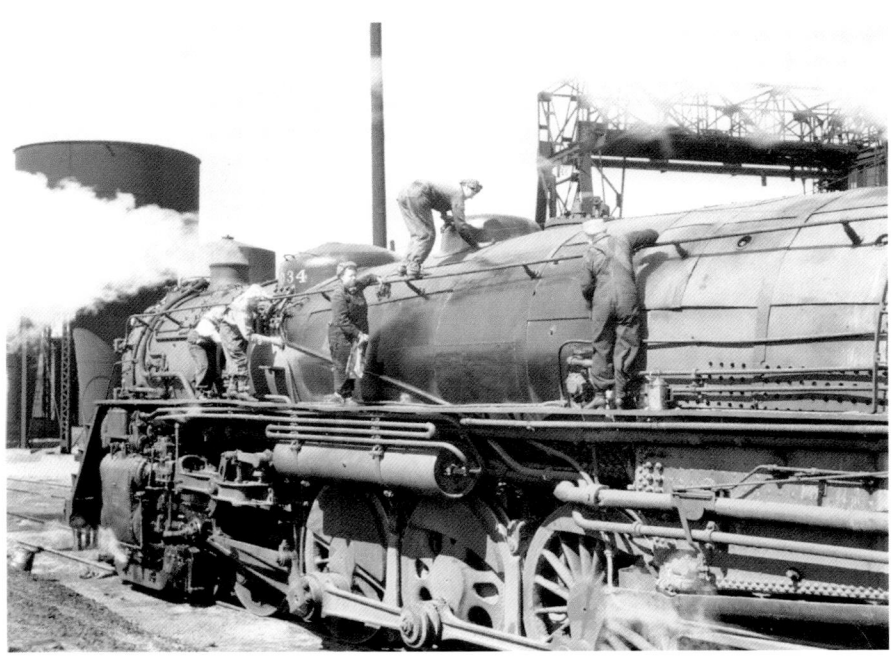

Steam engines required considerable maintenance with their heavy work schedules during the war. *Courtesy of the Library of Congress.*

In addition to buying bonds to support the war, Arlington Heights residents wanted to make sure that their sons, husbands and daughters knew that the village was still thinking of them. The Park Tavern in the village was run by Mar Johnson. A serviceman driving through town had stopped for a drink and when he left, he placed a savings bank cast in the shape of an army ambulance on the bar. Johnson decided it would be a good idea to collect spare change, and each week, an Arlington Heights soldier's name was drawn and stuck on the bar's bulletin board as "Honor Man of the Week." Whatever was collected in the bank was wired to that soldier. The bank also "traveled" to churches, veteran organizations and anyone else who wanted to contribute. By the end of the war, more than $4,000 from the traveling bank had been sent to 180 soldiers, and their acknowledgments were tacked to a large map on the bar's wall. They knew that they had not been forgotten.[37]

In all, forty-one Arlington Heights boys were lost to the war. There was also a group of soldiers who had mixed feelings about leaving the village. On May 4, 1944, trucks arrived at Building H on the grounds of the navy training air field at Central and Wilke Roads. Out of the vehicles piled a

Arlington Heights, Illinois

group of seventeen- to twenty-year-old German army prisoners of war from Rommel's Afrika Corps. They were housed in the two-story barracks with a soccer field laid out to the south. The entire complex was surrounded with barbed wire.

Every morning trucks from the Great Lakes Naval Training Station arrived and collected the POWs for labor details on the training base near the shore of Lake Michigan. Later, American officers discovered that some of the Germans were first-class mechanics, so the POWs were put to work servicing truck, car and even airplane engines. For pay, they received $21.80 a month in coupons good at the POW post exchange. Some POWs were hired to help harvest farmers' fields and they put aside enough cash money for their hours to contribute $650 to the American War Fund. On their bulletin board they posted: "By this contribution it will be shown to the American people that German prisoners of war are ready with the limited means at their disposal to support American relief organizations in the purpose of lending support to all persons who have fallen into misery and distress because of the war."[38]

Chapter 9

BABY BOOM AND BUILDING BOOM

By 1947, the two hundred POWs had been shipped back to Germany and the camp fell into disuse. The training aircraft were flown away and the land was declared excess by the navy. Arlington Heights wanted the land for an airport but could not close the deal. In a court action, the navy retained the land and leased it to the village for a general aviation airport and later a trailer park. By 1953, however, the Cold War had descended and Communist missiles were judged a threat to the United States by the military. On April 28, 1954, the army acquired the old POW camp from the navy and converted the site into the Eighty-sixth Antiaircraft Battalion (NIKE) for the recently activated Forty-fifth Antiaircraft Brigade, and leased two additional pockets of 5.78 and 6.98 acres southeast of the site on Illinois State Route 58. Construction of site C-80 was begun with the dual launching pits on the old navy land and the fire controls on the two small parcels of land. HHB, Eighty-sixth AAA Battalion and Battery A, became an operational missile battalion in March 1955. The hangar was the battalion and battery headquarters, the missile support shop, the mess hall (cooking was done outside in a tent) and barbershop. The "H" building was the barracks. Arlington Heights became part of the ring of NIKE missile launch sites protecting Chicago from Russian bombers.[39]

The late 1940s saw the soldiers return to the village, and residents who had scrimped and saved and rationed to support the war all wanted to enjoy the fruits of victory. Many put down roots and became familiar fixtures in the community. Carl Weinrich, the air raid warden, learned the shoe repair trade from his father and opened his own store in 1946 in a wooden building on Dunton Avenue and then moved to Campbell Street. He prospered there for thirty years until he settled at 41 South Dunton. Except for four years when he served as village clerk, he worked in the central business district until his death in 2000. Carl's son David carried on the business until 2009.

The residents were eager to spend the money they had saved working overtime in the war materiels factories. Rationing was being lifted—although gradually—and the soldiers took advantage of the GI Bill of Rights that had been passed by Congress providing grants for college educations. The Veterans Administration provided low-cost loans to buy homes while developers took options on blocks of land to resume the building boom throttled by the Depression. Business at Arlington Heights banks became brisk. Shirley Brown found herself in the middle of the boom:

> *From 1947 to 1952 I worked at the Arlington Heights National Bank (what is now Chase bank) downtown. The town was growing and the bank couldn't handle the volume of trade anymore. The number of transactions were happening so fast that we had to put tables in the lobby to help handle all the trade. Imagine, you're sitting out there with your money in the hall. People were trustworthy. I started out letting people in and out of the vault. Upstairs we had machines—you took the checks and deducted them from the accounts. There were 5 of us doing that all the time.*

Except for the WPA projects like Recreation Park, infrastructure and redecoration make-work, the village had stagnated, remaining basically the same as when growth had slowed in 1930. In 1947, its population had stalled at about 5,700. At that time, Dr. Robert Muench moved into rooms at 9 East Campbell Street above the block of buildings formed by the small post office, a barbershop, meat market and the real estate offices of Krause & Kehe. He remembers his impression of the small farming community:

> *It was fairly diverse with farming being the principal business. This included dairy farming, truck gardening, mushroom houses, nurseries and commodity crops like corn and soybeans. There was some light manufacturing such as the A.H. Seating Company and Creamery Packaging. Commuters took the C&NW into Chicago and an assortment of local businesses and professions comprised the main working population.*
>
> *The center of the community was a small cluster of buildings occupying the triangular lot at Vail and Davis Streets—where the Jewel store is today—Our town council met in the courtroom of the triangular village building. The fire department, police station and jail were in the back.*
>
> *The business district back then was divided by the railroad tracks and Northwest Highway. It (the north side of the tracks) featured Loretta's*

Baby Boom and Building Boom

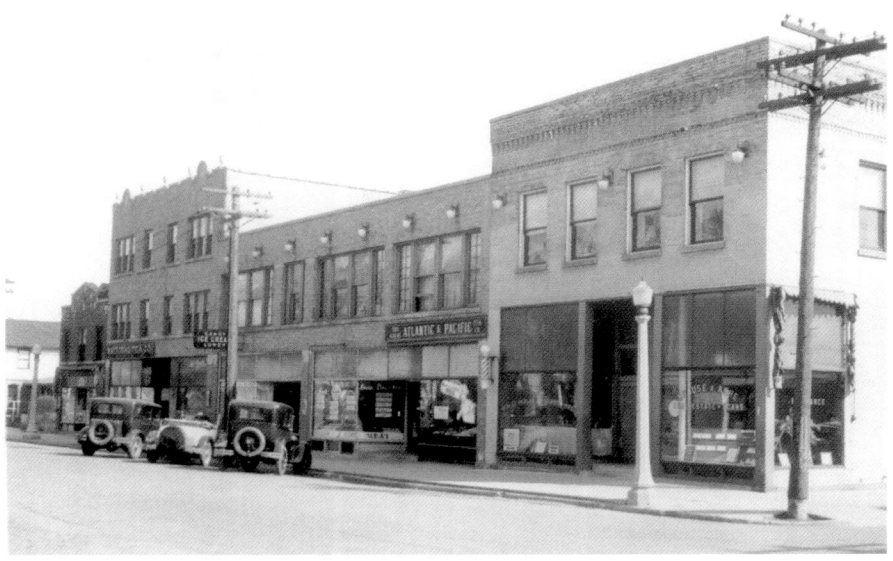

The Krause & Kehe loan office (far right) anchored Campbell Street corner in the 1930s. *Courtesy of Val Novak.*

> *Tavern-Restaurant and the Arlington Theater on Evergreen Street. A hardware store, Lohr's pharmacy and Carsten's Funeral Home were along Northwest Highway. On the south side of the tracks was the principal business district including the First Arlington National Bank, Sieberg's Drug Store, Hagenbring's Dry Goods, a five-and-ten-cents store and assorted small business enterprises. Our food came from the Jewel, National Tea and the A&P markets. The Lauterburg and Oehler Funeral Home was on Campbell Street.*

Medical care in the postwar village fell to a handful of family care doctors like Dr. Muench and very few specialists until years later. These physicians delivered as many as two thousand babies a year (hence the term "Baby Boom") at their peak. Dr. Muench remembers, "We did surgery, pediatrics, geriatrics, orthopedics and family counseling. It was pretty much a 'cradle-to-grave' type of work and I loved it." His daily practice ranged from hospitalizing a few children during the polio scare in the 1950s to working in the small clinic at the racetrack and treating transient workers on the farms. "A neighbor lady called and said her daughter was in terrible pain and might die. I went over and delivered a nice baby boy. Mama said 'I just thought she was getting fat.'"[40]

Arlington Heights, Illinois

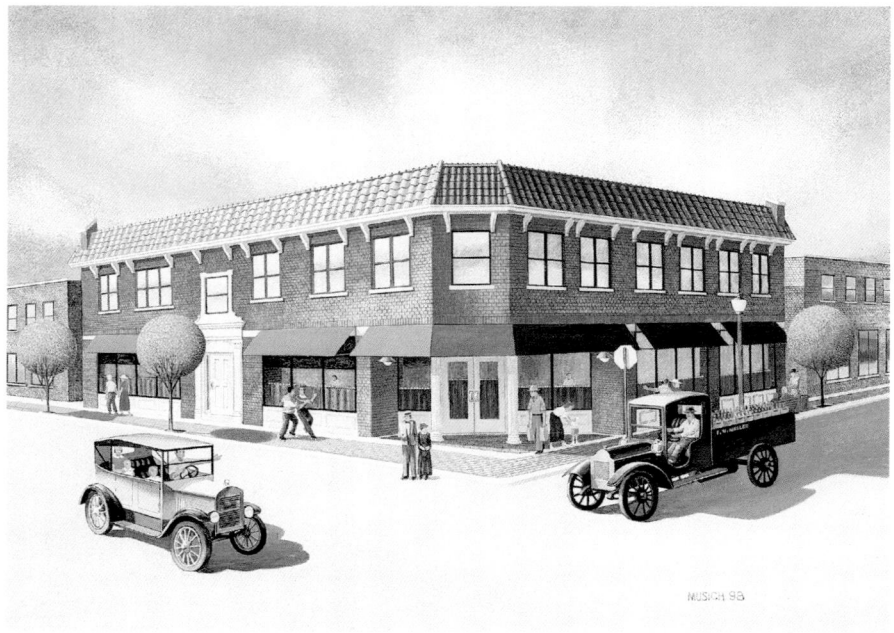

Hagenbring's store, Campbell and Vail. The store started as a five-and-dime in the 1920s and operated until the early 1990s. A restaurant and the Metropolis Performing Arts Centre now adjoin this site. *Painting by Jack Musich.*

While Dr. Muench was setting up his practice in 1947, builders, developers, eager buyers and con men were descending upon the village. Acres of farmland beckoned and the zoning seemed flexible for a variety of construction schemes. The auto industry was returning to civilian production; new layaway and down-payment plans became available and the men flooded back into the workforce, largely displacing the women who had taken their place for the war's duration. The search for the "American Dream" was alive and well in Arlington Heights: work in Chicago, live in a pretty house with a green lawn and 2.5 children. But the early responders created immediate problems that would affect the village for the next ten years.

In the 1940s, most streets in Arlington Heights were oiled dirt. The village halted all new streets until construction codes could be drawn up requiring better roads for the long haul. Donna Turek's father had to struggle with these conditions and she remembers one of his resourceful—if dangerous—solutions: "My father drove a truck for Sterling Oil in the early 1940s. In the winter when the highway wasn't plowed, he used to drive down the train tracks in order to get the fuel oil to people's homes further down in

Baby Boom and Building Boom

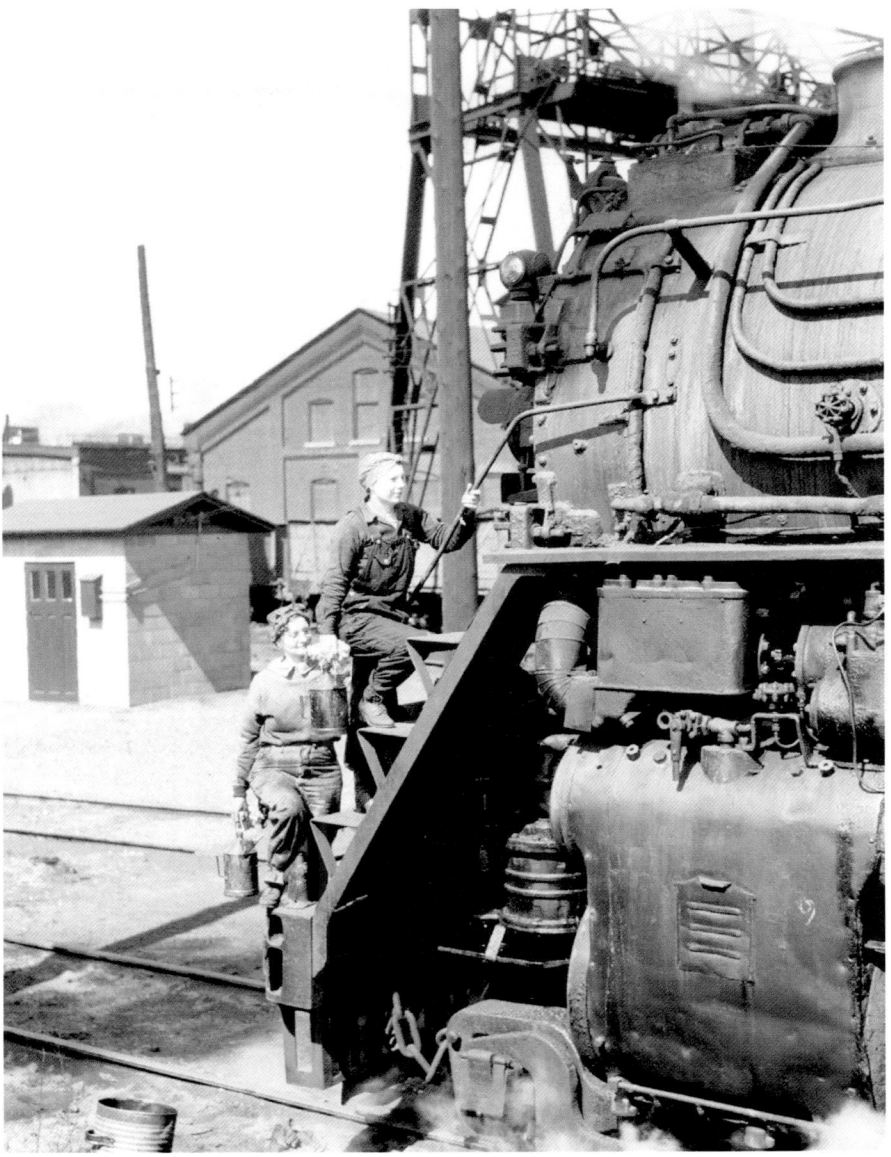

Women working as wipers on a steam locomotive during World War II. *Courtesy of the Library of Congress.*

Arlington Heights, Illinois

Arlington. He knew the schedule so he avoided the trains long enough to drive where he had to go."

Developers bought up acres of farmlands for construction, claiming that new buyers would want lots of elbow room. The board did not want new homes to rely on septic fields when they were built near the new sewers that would generate revenue from use fees. Some homes were built right atop old septic fields, which were hardly stable platforms. Disturbing the fields that had been used for the disposal of solid waste also created problems when rain and hot summers encouraged an "open sewer" aroma to rise from the excavations. Neighbors also bombarded the besieged board with complaints of gasoline engines running loudly at all hours blowing hot air to dry plaster.

As new buyers drove up and down the barren streets peering at "for sale" signs, they were waved over by "salesmen" with picture books of the new homes to be built for the lucky few who got their down payment of $500 to $2,000 registered first. The amount requested generally depended on the age of the sucker's car. These con artists often sold the same home or home site many times to different people and skipped town with all the down payment money. Early on, builders tried to keep construction costs down to $10,000. However, wartime price controls that had been clamped on building materials were removed and the cost of lumber, nails and wire rose steeply. The median family income in 1947 was $1,400.[41] A minimum cash payment for a house, determined by the lending companies and banks, was about $5,000. This amount today in modern dollars would be about $48,553.

Some returning GIs bought a parcel of land but could not afford to build a house, so they built a garage on the property and lived in it. In 1946, the zoning board was besieged. Permits were issued for building 158 homes, 3 stores, 1 factory, garages and house additions amounting to roughly $2.1 million in construction. By 1947, that number had jumped to 210 homes in Laurenwood and Scarsdale developments. Unincorporated Scarsdale Estates added another 30 residences. More than 200 homes were built in 1948 and new commercial construction brought that year's total to $3.1 million worth of work on village land.

A new building code was adopted. Virtually all the homes built had been two stories, some with finished first floors and unfinished second floors to be completed by the homeowner. But less expensive one-story ranch-style houses appeared and once again protests were heard from neighborhoods. By 1949, veterans who had built garages to live in or deposited mobile homes on their property received eviction notices. "Row houses" and what

Baby Boom and Building Boom

came to be known as "tract houses"—all resembling one another and made of prefabricated units nailed and screwed together—were forbidden.

During a meeting attended by seven hundred residents in 1950, a moratorium was demanded, shutting down further development of the surrounding farmland until the village infrastructure—waste disposal, water supply, electrical distribution, fire and police protection—could be upgraded to match village growth. What followed was a seesaw battle among neighborhood residents, developers and elected village officials as building permits were granted and withheld on a case-by-case basis.

Experimentation continued as fields were leveled and gouged out for new construction. Trucraft Homes built low-cost ranch-style houses down North Beverly Avenue between Frederick Street and Oakton Avenue. Around the corner and down both sides of Frederick Street, two-story Cape Cod homes with finished first floors and unfinished second (for the home handyman) ones were built during the early 1950s. A few unique Lustron Homes were made of two-foot-square steel panels both bolted and welded together. To hang a picture required only affixing a magnet with a hook to the wall. Even the metal roof panels were designed to resemble shingles—except for the

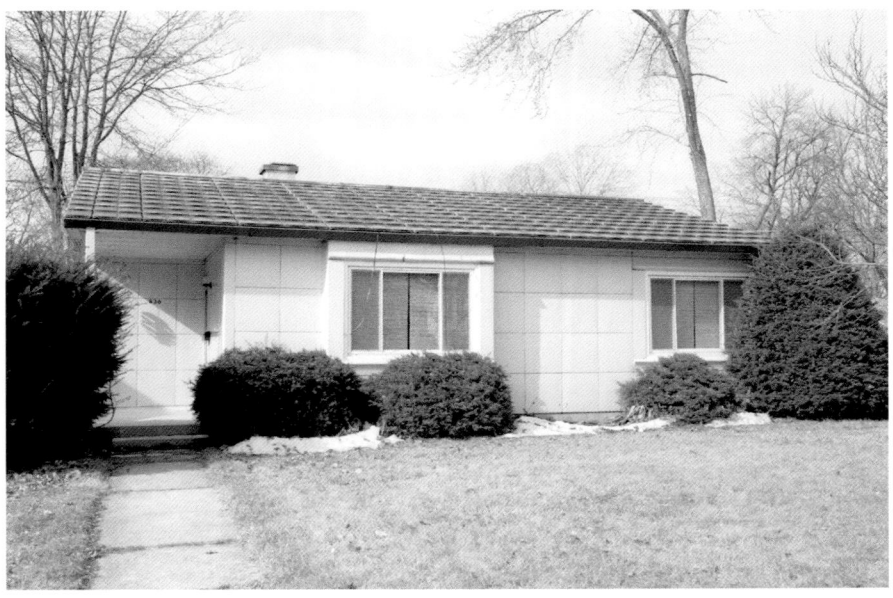

Lustron home, 1950s. The exterior is made up of yellow metal tiles and is considered extremely energy-efficient. The interior walls are also steel, requiring only magnets to hang pictures. *Photo by Gerry Souter.*

shine. Some intrepid handymen built homes from kits they had purchased from Sears Roebuck and Montgomery Ward catalogues.

To service this flurry of new homes, the village dug deep wells and pumping stations in neighborhoods, providing hard water that left coatings of white lime on fixtures. Homeowners had to buy water softeners to treat the water as it entered the home, requiring fifty-pound salt blocks or large sacks of salt pellets to remove the corrosive minerals. Insulation in most homes was basic rock wool blown in between the interior and exterior walls or hung in paper-sandwiched blankets. These fibers settled over time, leaving large un-insulated gaps where cold air could enter. Village building inspectors were kept busy spotting cheap shortcuts used by contractors. This vigilance left Arlington Heights with the most stringent building code in the northwest suburbs.

Despite the often indifferent construction, real estate scams, rising costs of building materials and strain on the village infrastructure to keep up with this phenomenal growth, neighborhoods rose from meadows and former cornfields. Between 1946 and 1956, 4,015 homes were built with a value of about $60 million. This blossoming residential growth had little effect, unfortunately, on the downtown business district. While numerous small businesses came and went, the main commercial development moved northeast from the town center.[42]

Rand Road, the former military road running north on a diagonal from Chicago, gathered its own townships. One of these adjoining communities, Mount Prospect, provided the land for the first enclosed shopping mall in the region. Designed by noted commercial architect Victor Gruen, Randhurst Mall opened in 1962 to great hoopla. The building boom that lured families to the suburbs was lubricated by new roads that connected the communities, and downtown Arlington Heights parking could no longer handle even the dwindling number of customers. New "anchor" stores and malls with huge parking lots drew away the local business. Downtowns that had grown up around their train stations began to ossify and lose longtime commercial tenants. The end of the 1950s in Arlington Heights was greeted with the sounds of hammering, sawing and digging. However, the owners of the new houses—mostly commuters to jobs in Chicago—looked elsewhere for their goods and services.

Chapter 10

DOWNTOWN WAY DOWN—1960S ARLINGTON HEIGHTS

The Arlington High School Homecoming Parade was a big deal as it wound through the village streets in the 1940s and 1950s. Teenagers piled onto their own or their families' cars decorated with flags, ribbons and coils of twisted crepe paper, all predicting victory for the homecoming football game to be waged by the Arlington Cardinals. Village residents turned out and lined the curbs to cheer on their offspring and show support for their namesake high school. Pat Gieseke Winkelman remembers:

> In a photo from homecoming parade in 1951, that was my future husband's car. That's what we would do every year—we'd take the boyfriend's car [Kenneth Winkelman] and that year I was driving. I wasn't a very good driver at that point. I got my driver's license at the village hall in Arlington Heights on Wing Street and Vail Avenue. The day I took my driver's test I did not know how to drive, but I took my dad's brand new car there all by myself—the parents didn't have to come with you. I was just as nervous as could be. Son of a gun if I didn't pass that test. I learned how to drive afterward.[43]

The parade rolled across the railroad tracks, led by police on motorcycles, and the Arlington High School Band tootled and pounded the catchy traditional marches. As the band snaked back to the school, the music faded down Euclid Street and sleepy silence once again returned to the downtown business district. The continuing festivities only flared briefly in the restaurant bars and drugstores where watchers and boosters could down a beer or a cream soda float before heading home.

As the home building wars raged in the village boardrooms, the downtown business district quietly simmered in the smoky fall sun as leaves were raked

Arlington Heights, Illinois

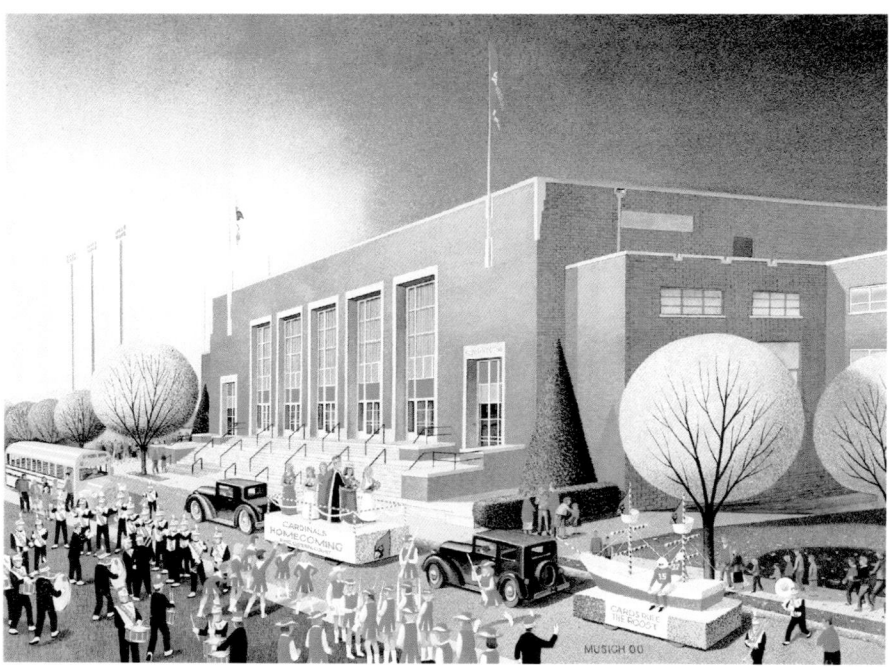

Arlington High School homecoming parade. This was a huge event in the village. *Painting by Jack Musich.*

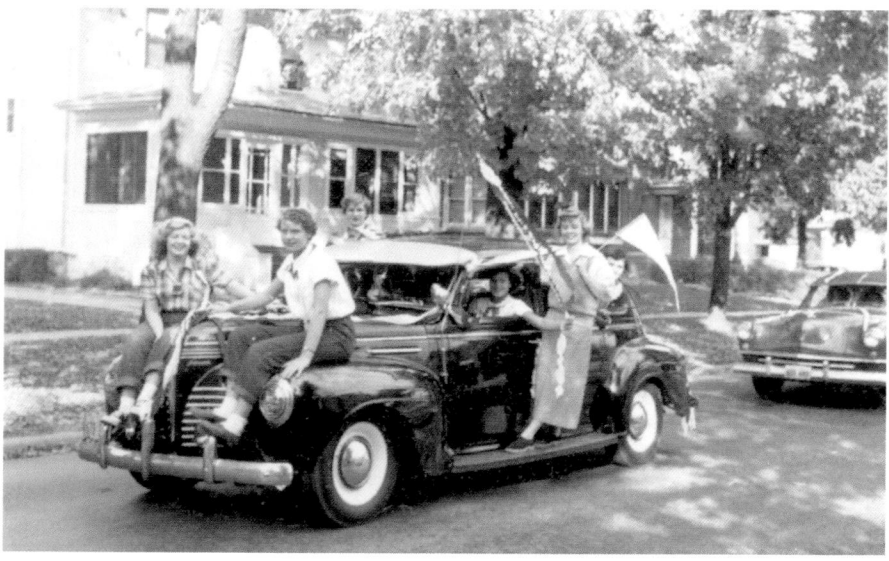

Homecoming parade, 1951. Pat Gieseke is driving the car belonging to her boyfriend and future husband, Kenneth Winkelman. *Courtesy of Pat Gieseke Winkelman.*

Downtown Way Down—1960s Arlington Heights

into piles on the side streets for burning. The automobile and the new housing developments had entirely changed the character of the former farm community. People still visited the town center because the banks were there, as were the village offices, but the many shops watched customers stream down Euclid Avenue and Kensington Street to the Randhurst Mall, or farther afield to Golf Mill or Old Orchard. The automobile and four-lane paved roads made these trips so easy.

On the edge of the business district, the Arlington Market opened on Dryden Avenue and Kensington Street in 1958. This area had been used by local teens and some adults as an informal auto racetrack and demolition derby with junker cars. The mall was open but followed the pattern of one or two "anchor" stores surrounded by small merchandise and service shops. This one-stop mall also featured a bank and Polk Brothers Appliance store. Shirley Brown remembers the area well:

> *After the war was over, my father and another guy started S&S Woodworkers on Beverly Lane. They made millwork. They built Beverly Lanes Bowling Alley in that building and when they heard about the Arlington Market going up they thought it would be shaped so that the bowling alley would be right in the middle. But it was built the other way. I remember when you could dump your refuse there. And that's what Arlington Market is built on—a dump.*

Ironically, the railroad had been responsible for access to William Dunton's prairie town that grew to become Arlington Heights, but now that same access was diminishing the heart of the community. In the 1960s, Interstate Route 90 was extended past Arlington Heights to the south. As with the railroad, the village lobbied the state to build an unplanned off-ramp from the interstate onto Arlington Heights Road. By this time the village had annexed unincorporated land out to Algonquin and Golf Roads, which were already commercially zoned. Malls and corporate headquarters began digging in and started another growth area on the southern edge of Arlington Heights. The village was now sandwiched between two major commercial shopping strips and bisected by access roads that acted as conduits through town to where the shopping action was found.

One thriving enterprise located today near the town's southern border is the Mitsuwa Marketplace, a complex featuring Oriental cuisine, beers, sake, videos, books and gifts. That's not so unusual now, but retired businessman Gerald Beauvais remembers a day in the early 1960s when he helped entertain some Japanese visitors:

ARLINGTON HEIGHTS, ILLINOIS

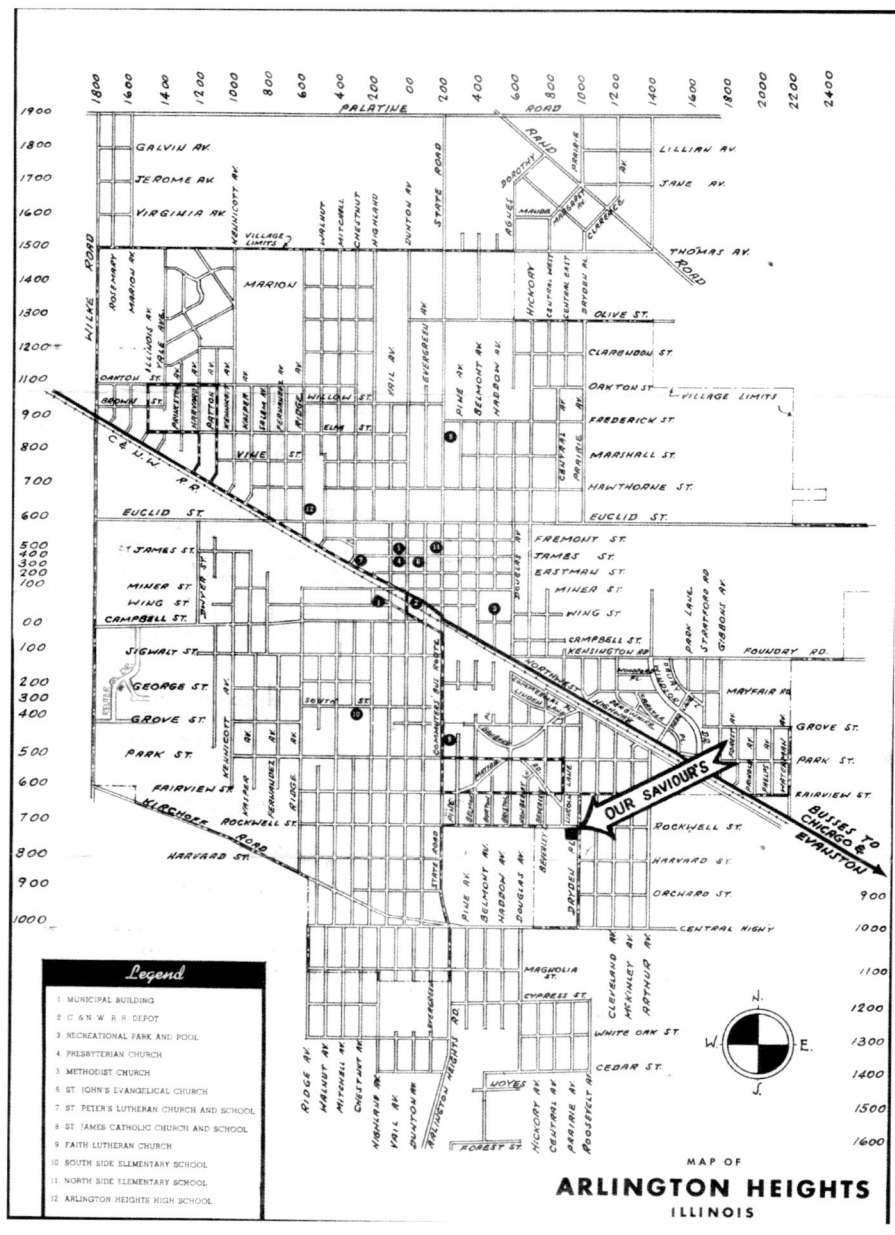

A planning map of Arlington Heights in 1959. *Courtesy of Arlington Heights Public Works.*

Downtown Way Down—1960s Arlington Heights

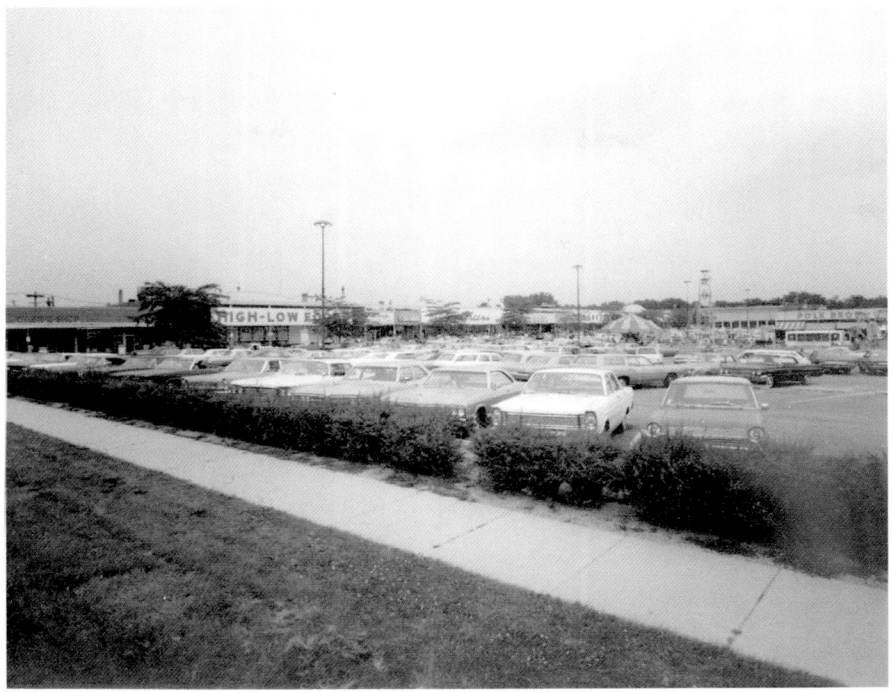

Arlington Market, 1970. The market was built in 1958 to accommodate the growing need for shopping facilities in the burgeoning village. The majority of buildings (except for Eros Restaurant, a bank and a fast-food restaurant) were torn down in the early 2000s for a housing complex. As of this writing, construction has been delayed, due to the shrinking economy. *Courtesy of Arlington Heights Public Works.*

> *I was a member of the Arlington Heights Jaycees. There was a group of Japanese Jaycees visiting in Chicago and a friend of mine wanted to show them what life was like in the suburbs. We made arrangements to meet them near Prospect High School. A police escort took them through the Greenbrier subdivision, Randhurst Mall, and then out to the race track. We had no time to see the whole race, but they stood by the rail as the horses came around the first quarter turn; then we were off to city hall where Mayor Woods made them honorary citizens and they were given a demonstration of the fire department's new ladder truck. We had a big party that night at my house; it broke up about 11:30 p.m. Next morning, garbage from the party was five feet high.*

While the downtown began suffering commercial ennui, its administrative core was improved in 1960 with a new village hall built at the corner of

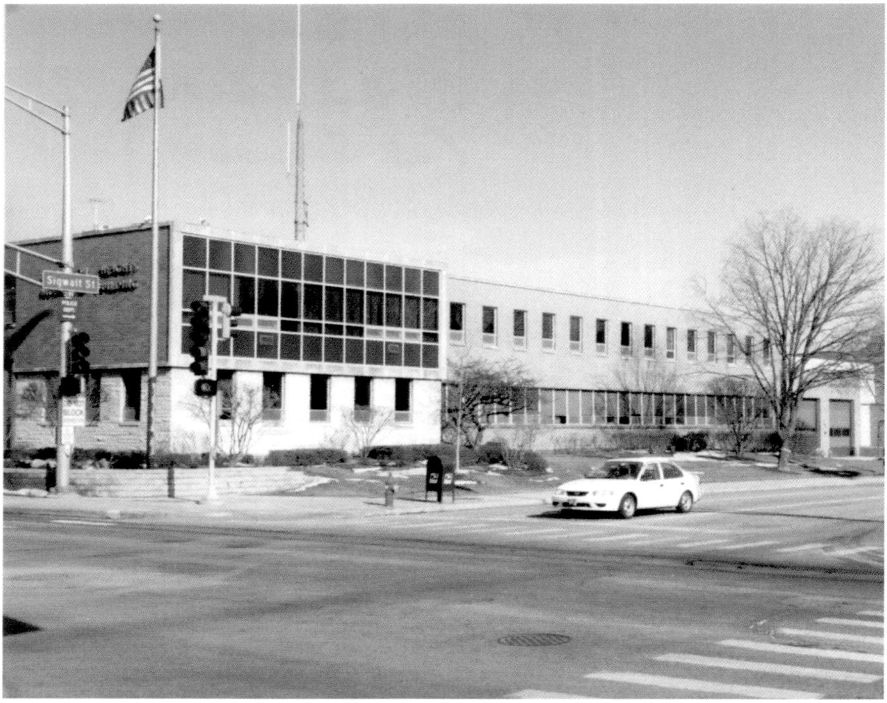

Arlington Heights, Illinois

Arlington Heights Village Hall, 1960s. *Courtesy of Arlington Heights Public Works.*

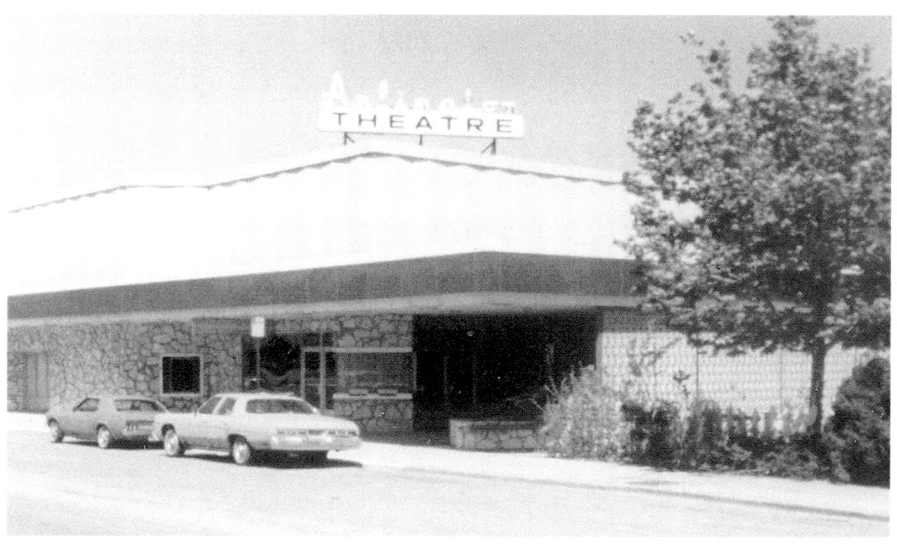

Arlington Theater just prior to its closing, 1980s. *Helen Horath estate.*

Downtown Way Down—1960s Arlington Heights

Arlington Heights Road and Sigwalt Street. But as new structures rose, others vanished. The roller mill that had been a fixture for almost one hundred years, grinding farmers' crops into flour and meal, was torn down to provide a parking lot for the new Arlington Theater movie house. Gieseke's Department Store on Davis Street, the pride of a family that went back to the turn of the century, closed its doors.

With the assassination of President John F. Kennedy, the murder of Reverend Martin Luther King Jr. and the killing of presidential candidate Robert Kennedy, the 1960s became the age of rage. The war in Vietnam blossomed as the alleged attacks on U.S. Navy vessels by North Vietnamese gunboats justified the landing of Marines on a Danang beach in 1965. Back in the United States, the civil rights injustices in the South and the North during the 1960s and '70s drew opposing crowds into bloody confrontations. Once again, because of its location away from the city and its strong conservative voting record, Arlington Heights became both a challenge and apparently low-hanging fruit for the anti-radical right. One example in 1972 demonstrates this dichotomy.

Arlington High School had created a Student Forum monitored by Principal Bruno Waara. The forum invited a member of the radical group the Black Panthers to speak. When a student called in to Howard Miller's morning radio talk show to inquire if the Black Panthers were indeed coming to Arlington High School, the broadcast alerted a huge wave of opposition. A Prospect Heights minister, Reverend Paul Lindstrom, threatened to have his congregation picket the school to protest the Panthers. Angry parents lit up the school's switchboard. Finally, Waara gave up and the invitation was canceled. To fill in, another speaker was invited, Mr. Frank Collins, who happened to be the leader of the American Nazi Party. He showed up in full uniform, Nazi armband and all. Ironically, very few parents, students or religious leaders opposed Collins's appearance.[44]

It seemed everything that was familiar was caught up in a cascade of change. In the business district, some changes were better than others. Commuters to Chicago discovered their world transformed overnight on May 11, 1956. The C&NW Railroad had done its best to keep up with the revolution in America's transportation needs. The Interstate Highway System had been created by President Dwight Eisenhower, ostensibly for military purposes to allow strategic goods to be quickly transported to either coast. These high-speed concrete roads allowed trucking to overtake railroads as the prime mover of non-commodity freight. The interstate's eight-lane paved expressways also extended the range of new, faster automobiles, allowing long drives made in comfort. This cut into fading passenger train service, already crippled by the growing popularity of commercial aviation.

Arlington Heights, Illinois

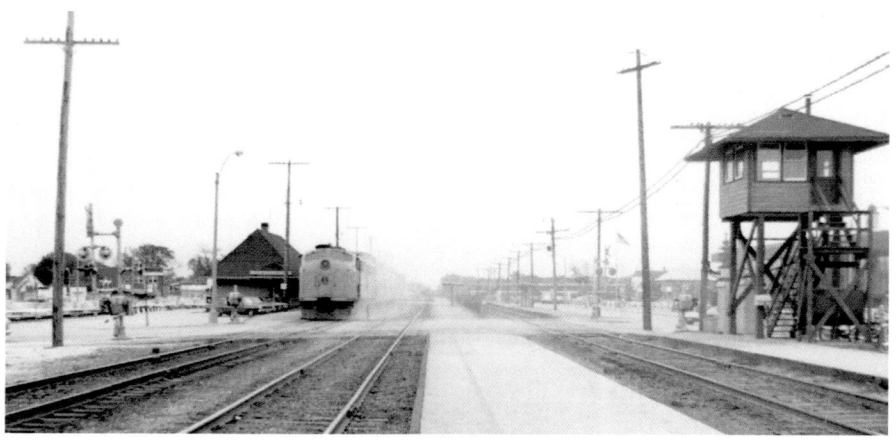

A diesel train pulling into the Arlington Heights train station, 1950s. *Courtesy of the Arlington Heights Planning Commission.*

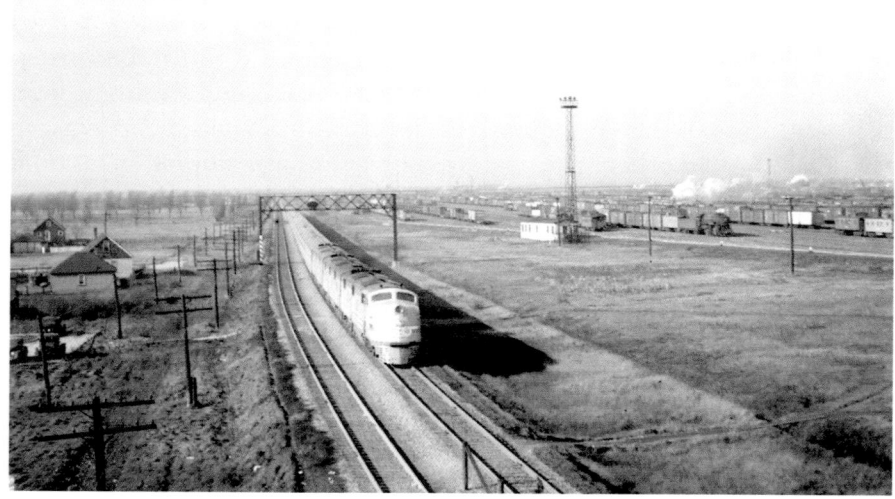

A diesel train, 1940s. These diesel-electric locomotives began replacing steam engines because of lower operating costs and cheaper construction. *Courtesy of the Library of Congress.*

By 1956, the "Cheap & Nothing Wasted" line was convinced that steam engines hauling the commuter trains into Chicago and back had outlived their usefulness. Steam power, which had ruled the rails since the 1820s, was high maintenance, spewed coal smoke and produced tons of ashes, and the locomotives themselves were expensive to build. Diesel locomotives were

Downtown Way Down—1960s Arlington Heights

quickly replacing the old teakettles because they were cheap to run, cheap to build and easier to repair. The C&NW scraped together every diesel loco from its entire system between Wisconsin and Clinton, Iowa. On that fateful May day, steam engines took commuters from Arlington Heights to Chicago, but diesel locomotives brought them home in the evening. The swap was an amazing feat of logistics.

Motive power was not the only improvement to make commuters and business people happy. The charming landscaping that formed Railroad Park around the original 1892 passenger station—which had shrunk considerably by the 1950s because of endless remodeling—was finally dug up and chopped down to provide more parking for cars. The train ride was improved with new coaches. Commuter trains had always received hand-me-downs from the C&NW mainline passenger service. These steel "heavyweight" coaches that had replaced the old wooden firetraps by the 1940s were still no bargain. They were drafty—relying on open windows for air circulation—and though they were heated by steam produced by the locomotive, passengers' feet cooked while their heads froze in the winter. Seats were either covered with horsehair—which retained the "trace" of the last person to sit there, especially on damp and hot days—or wicker, which had problems of its own. Smoking was permitted in all coaches, producing a pungent, eye-stinging effluvia, especially when mixed with the soot and ash blowing in through the open windows. These clanking throwbacks were finally replaced with streamlined stainless steel and aluminum cars offering sealed windows, air conditioning, comfortable, serviceable upholstery and one smoking car per train. Coupled behind a relatively quiet diesel locomotive that did not spray soot in all directions amid clouds of steam and smoke, these new coaches transformed the commuter experience.[45]

Another phenomenon exerting its influence on the downtown business district was the two-car garage. By the 1950s, a generation of residents had never sat astride a horse or steered a span of horses in the traces of a flatbed wagon. Like the outhouse, the horse stable had vanished and in its place was the garage for the family car. The new affluence that came with the postwar boom and the shift of the job market commute to Chicago via automobile created the need for two cars in a family. This doubled the traffic in downtown Arlington Heights on weekends as mom and dad ran separate errands. The latest auto generation of teenagers wanted car ownership while they were still in high school. If dad drove to work, then mom was no longer stranded at home. Parking facilities became as important as the goods and services offered—and the outlying malls offered acres of free parking.

Arlington Heights, Illinois

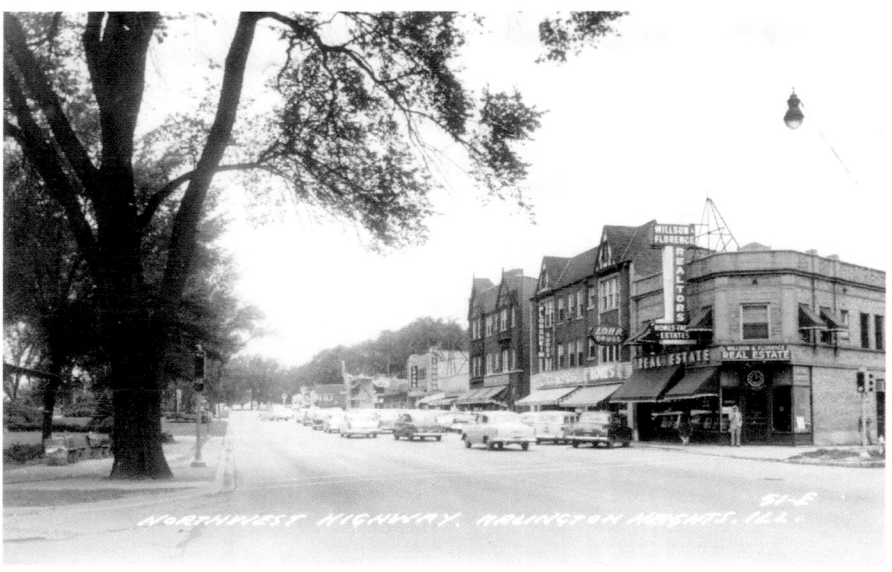

Northwest Highway, 1950s. *Courtesy of Jodee Lohr Gieseke.*

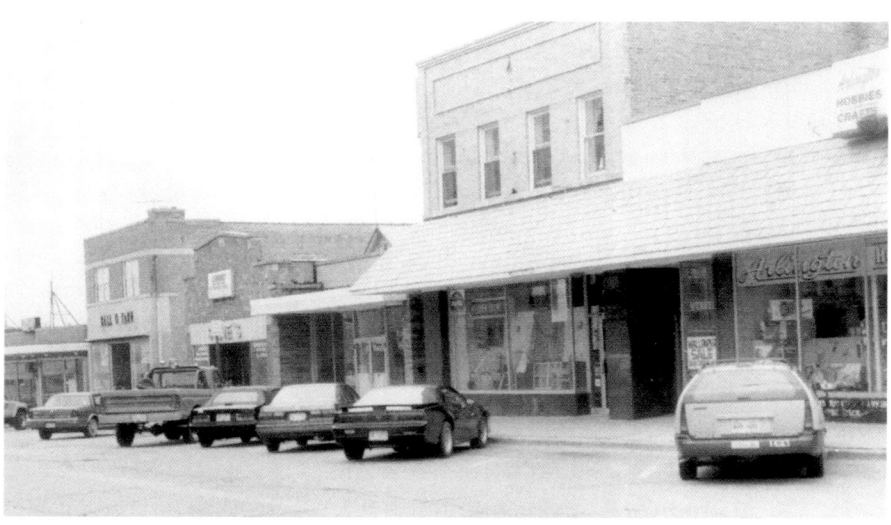

Dunton Avenue, north of Northwest Highway, 1980s. Most of these businesses are now boarded up and are slated to be replaced by a condominium complex. *Courtesy of the Arlington Heights Planning Commission.*

Downtown Way Down—1960s Arlington Heights

Arlington Heights parking was still based on the horse-drawn buggy, where the wagons clopped to a stop with their equine motive power's nose to the curb's hitching post and water trough. By the 1950s and '60s, that horse-and-buggy diagonal parking holdover persisted.

Chapter 11

PROTECTION AND PREVENTION GROW WITH THE VILLAGE

Fire protection had come a long way since the days of the bully boys of the volunteer fire brigade galloping with Old Faithful to a burning farmstead and dipping the hose into a convenient creek. The town fire bell had finally been replaced by telephone alerts and then two-way radios after World War II. The natty uniforms and caps gave way to more utilitarian "bunker" gear and full-time firefighters were being considered. By 1924, the fire department had grown to twenty-six men, including Chief Arthur Volz. In 1928, a six-hundred-gallon-per-minute pumper was added to the roster, and by 1940 the first class of first aid trainees had graduated. And yet, for all the growth, the department was still a volunteer fire brigade. In 1942, firemen/shopkeepers received one dollar for each alarm to which they responded. If it was a false alarm, they got nothing. The chief got five dollars for showing up and the lieutenants received three dollars each.

That year also tested the men when the Creamery Package plant went up in flames. Liquid tallow that was applied to the tin milk cans fed the fire into an inferno. The smoke was dense, but the company managed to dowse the fire before it reached the main building. Also, by 1942, the war overseas was heating up and a twenty-four-member auxiliary fire department was created as a Civil Defense measure. All the men were above draft age, and at the close of the war, four of them elected to join the fire department.

It was 1947 when the last volunteer fire chief signed on. Chief Elroy J. Winkelman replaced thirty-year veteran Richard H. Jahn. From there the department became a mix of full-time and volunteer firefighters. New types of apparatus and new procedures had to be mastered in classes that led to the creation of the Arlington Heights Fire Academy, one of few such institutions in the country. Neighboring communities sent their firemen to the academy for training and certification.

During his tenure as chief, Winkelman also fell victim to firehouse tradition. Since the days when horses had galloped through town hauling pumpers and ladder trucks to fires, firemen were accustomed to living close to their equine partners. In addition to the pampered horses, cats roamed the stables, dealing with the rats that infested the hay bins and sacks of oats. But the firehouse dog was considered an integral part of firefighting tradition. His job was to race ahead of the horse-drawn apparatus, barking and clearing the roadway. That job went away with gasoline-powered fire engines and their blaring sirens. The dog remained as a mascot who often rode to fires on the ladder truck.

Shortly after the Arlington Heights Fire Department became a full-time operation, one of the men brought a dog named Suzie to the station to serve as the mascot. The loveable mutt enjoyed the freedom of the station for about a week, and then Chief Winkelman showed up one morning. Suzie's ears went back at the sight of the stranger, and she yapped at his heels and chased the fire boss from the station. Shortly thereafter, Suzie was canned as "Official Station Fire Dog." In 1973, a pooch once again took up residence—a Dalmatian presented as a gift. He was named Harvey and in his youth he rode to all the calls. He logged more time at the department than any fireman to that time: fourteen years for twenty-four hours a day, 365 days a year.[46]

Sharing the back end of the village hall with the fire station was the police department. From the early days of the village until the turn of the century, policing was hit or miss. There was no jail with cells until the 1890s, and the job floated between night watchmen and part-time day men until 1907, when Officer Arthur Dieball took the oath for a trial six-month period for forty-eight dollars a month. He lasted a little longer than a year.

By the 1920s, Arlington Heights was besieged by automobilists "scorching" through town half crocked on bootleg gin. Fights broke out when illegal stills were raided. Unsavory types and drug users showed up with the new Arlington Park Racecourse. Domestic abuse soared in construction workers' shanty towns and tramps wandered the town's side streets, breaking into homes and rummaging in garbage cans. Chicago crime bosses fought over the "right" to sell illegal booze in local bars and roadhouses. They waged violent battles for slot machine and punchboard profits and bought up vacant houses to build stills for Chicago distribution. The village needed a modern police force.

Early crime reporting was primitive at best. A clerk answered the police station telephone number 6, and if an officer was needed immediately, a whistle attached to steam pumps was activated on the village hall roof. The policeman, on hearing the sonic blast, called the station from the nearest telephone for directions to the crime scene. Motorcycles were the police transport of choice, but in 1924, Officer Fred J. Koerber fatally plowed into a cement truck and

Protection and Prevention Grow with the Village

the other motorcycle policeman, Jack Claussen, resigned. The legendary Carl Herbert Skoog was hired. With previous motorcycle experience, the twenty-seven-year-old officer stepped into the job of Arlington Heights top cop in 1925, just in time for Prohibition violations to really heat up.[47]

Starting in 1926, Roger Touhy and his gang took over the beer-brewing market in Cook County. Each barrel of illegal beer cost about $4.50 to produce and was worth $55 to sell. Between 1927 and 1932, when Prohibition was repealed, twenty-seven incidents involving illegal alcohol were logged by Officer Skoog and his men in Arlington Heights.[48] Eventually, after outwitting the feds and eluding death threats from Capone's associates, Touhy was bundled off to prison. When he next emerged in 1956, he had a few moments to reflect on the Chicago mob's long memory just before a double-barrel shotgun almost cut him in two.

Over the decades from law enforcement's humble start in the 1920s until its peak with the purchase of a 1929 Plymouth Sedan, complete with red light and siren, the police department matured considerably. Two-way radios replaced the whistle-and-telephone crime reporting system, eventually achieving full ISPERN (Illinois State Police Emergency Radio Network) connectivity and a computer console in each of the town's fleet of police cruisers. In the 1960s, growth and training requirements demanded larger quarters. Under the leadership of Chief Robert P. Dierks, the current modern facility covering forty-four thousand square feet was built in the mid-1970s, complete with a state-of-the-art communications center, pistol range, classrooms and lock-up and administration offices. During that period and into the 1980s, Arlington Heights expanded its tax base with the annexation of Arlington Park. There was also an influx of gang-related incidents as families moved from Chicago to the suburbs and their offspring brought gang affiliations along with them. With the additional tax money, the Arlington Heights Police Department was able to add personnel and organize specialized units to combat the increase in gang-related crime.

The partnership between Arlington Heights and the Arlington Park Racecourse was severely tested at 1:30 a.m. on July 31, 1985, when a fire broke out in the post and paddock building next to the racetrack's grandstand. By 2:19 a.m., the fire department was on the scene, but the building was fully alight and eventually five alarms were required to bring enough equipment into the fight. As water cannons hammered their streams into the billowing clouds of gray smoke and firemen chopped their way into the structure, hidden flames burst into the open. Explosive experts from Fort Sheridan were called in to blast a trench and stop the spreading inferno, but by the time they arrived there was no chance to save the building or the entire grandstand structure.

Arlington Heights, Illinois

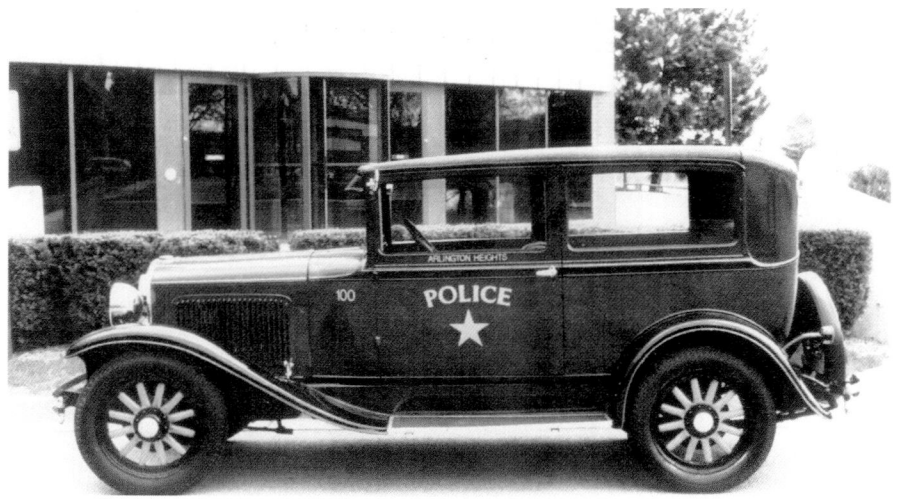

This Arlington Heights police car, a 1929 Plymouth, was purchased in 1930. *Courtesy of the Arlington Heights Police Department.*

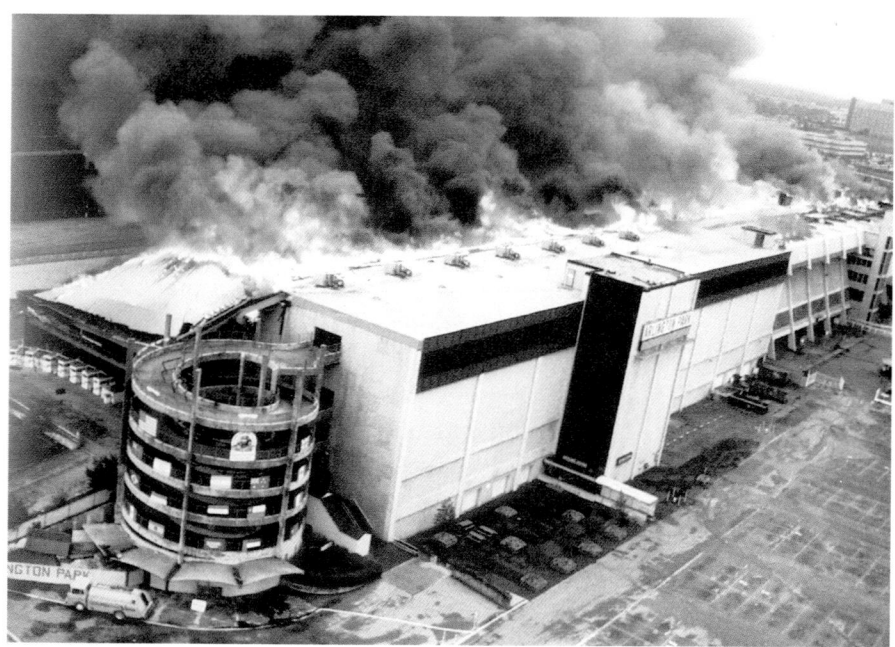

Arlington Park fire, 1985. *Courtesy of the Arlington Park Racecourse.*

Protection and Prevention Grow with the Village

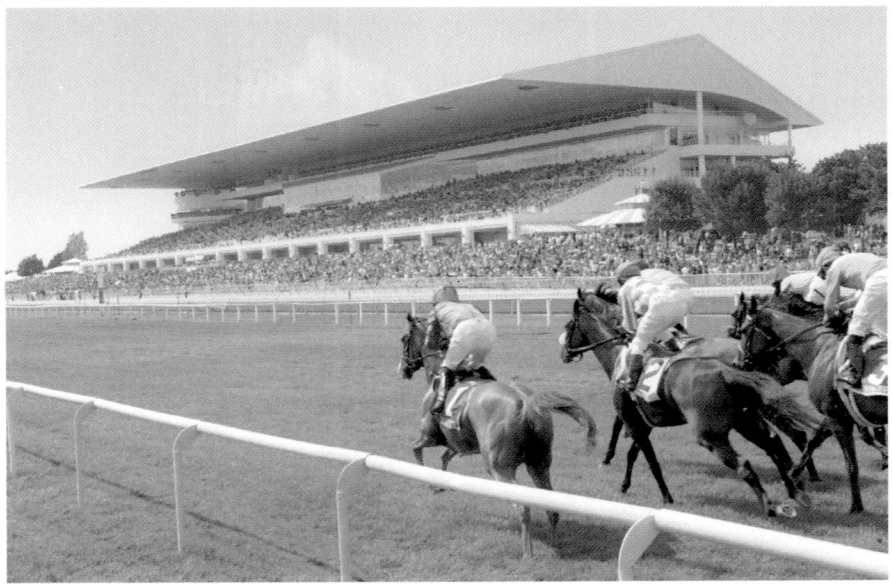

The new grandstand from the grass track at Arlington Park Racecourse in the 1990s. *Courtesy of the Arlington Park Racecourse.*

The track had been under new ownership for only two years and now it lay in ruins. Richard Duchossois, the principal investor, realized that the race meeting could be shifted to Hawthorn Park, but the big race of the year, the Arlington Budweiser-Million, faced cancellation. The Million had been running for four years and had built up an international reputation. The loss in revenue plus the loss of prestige was intolerable. Duchossois decided, on August 4, to run the race at Arlington Park despite the damages.

Trucks removed 250 loads of debris from the site daily. Hundreds of permits and documents had to be drafted as contractors came and went. Construction crews began work even as the debris was being removed. Arlington Heights village president James Ryan commented, "There is a sense of awe in what has happened and what is being done."

The August 25 Budweiser-Million came off with eight thousand of the thirty-five thousand fans seated on a makeshift grandstand and all the support facilities sheltered under forty-three red and white tents rigged on 271,000 square feet of new asphalt. The horse Teleprompter won a close finish over Greinton, and Arlington Heights's international reputation as a top venue in the world of horse racing was secure.[49] A new grandstand structure and multiuse convention space has been added to the original track plan.

Chapter 12

CONSTRUCTION AND DESTRUCTION GO HAND IN HAND

The "miracle" of the Arlington Budweiser-Million horse race was only a highlight in the decades from the 1970s to the 1990s as the village on the railroad tracks flailed about trying to find itself. The population continued to explode, reaching up toward fifty thousand. A bicycle ride to the C&NW train station put residents only forty-five minutes from their jobs in Chicago and the journey home in the evening was rewarded with a bar car in the center of the train. Drivers peeled off the I-90 Interstate onto Arlington Heights Road, or rolled down from jobs farther north on Rand Road. Corporate headquarters had risen from cornfields that had become too valuable to plant. Developers plunged along like baying hounds in pursuit of the crafty fox. Neighborhoods and paved streets pushed up from the fields, woods and reclaimed bogs crisscrossed with creeks and drainage ditches.

The village seemed to inherit the restlessness that had stirred its foundations back when it was young and smelled of raw timber, fresh paint and horse manure. This constant shape-shifting, repurposing and peripatetic meandering was commented on in print by architect Tom Seibert in *Arlington Heights, Chronicle of a Prairie Town* in 1997. His chapter on Arlington Heights architecture notes:

> *I have had a personal interest in one rather unusual facet of architecture... moving buildings. That was when I almost had to sell the excuse: "I can't get to work on time because there is a house blocking my driveway." Arlington Heights has quite a history of moving all types of buildings all over town. The reasons were sometimes even a little bizarre. The Elk Grove Methodist Church was moved twice because of noise from nearby taverns on Sundays.*

Arlington Heights, Illinois

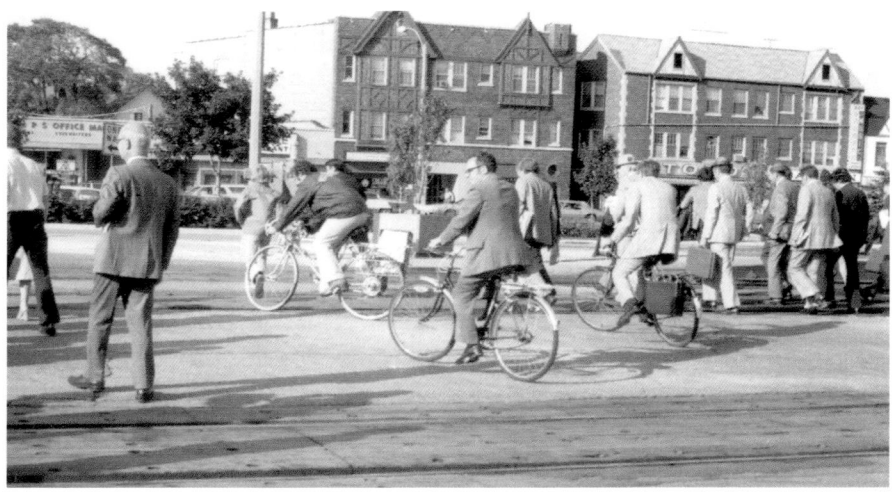

Commuters heading toward the train station, 1970s. Gas prices had soared and people found that bike riding added to physical fitness while lessening the number of trips to the pump. *Courtesy of the Arlington Heights Planning Commission.*

Of course, the first dwelling to hoist its skirts and head on down the road was William Dunton's two-story house built originally on the future site of the railroad tracks. It was moved to the east side of Arlington Heights Road (roughly the site of his bronze likeness in the little park that replaced the abandoned gas station at Arlington Heights Road and Northwest Highway). In 1905, it was hauled to 112 East Wing Street, and by 1935, its address was 705 East Hintz Road. It was finally flattened for a housing development in 1970.

Houses and commercial buildings seemed to have greater value in the past. Jacking up a residence and trundling it through the streets was not an obscure option. A house that once sat at 15 East Eastman Street started life at 15 South Evergreen Street in the early 1870s. When it was moved in 1885, a second story was added and it became a public hall. The first village hall in 1893 was built by Henry Luettge in 1880s at 101 West Davis and was sold to the village for $1,275. It was again sold to James Williams in 1914 when the new village hall was built at Vail Avenue and Wing Street. The former hall was moved to its present location at 925 North Dunton Avenue and the enclosed porch was added.

Another public building that went private once sat at 212 North Dunton Avenue. It started life as the village's first school at the corner of Miner Street and Evergreen Avenue. When the most recent shell laid over the old house was torn away, members of the Arlington Heights Historical Society were

Construction and Destruction Go Hand in Hand

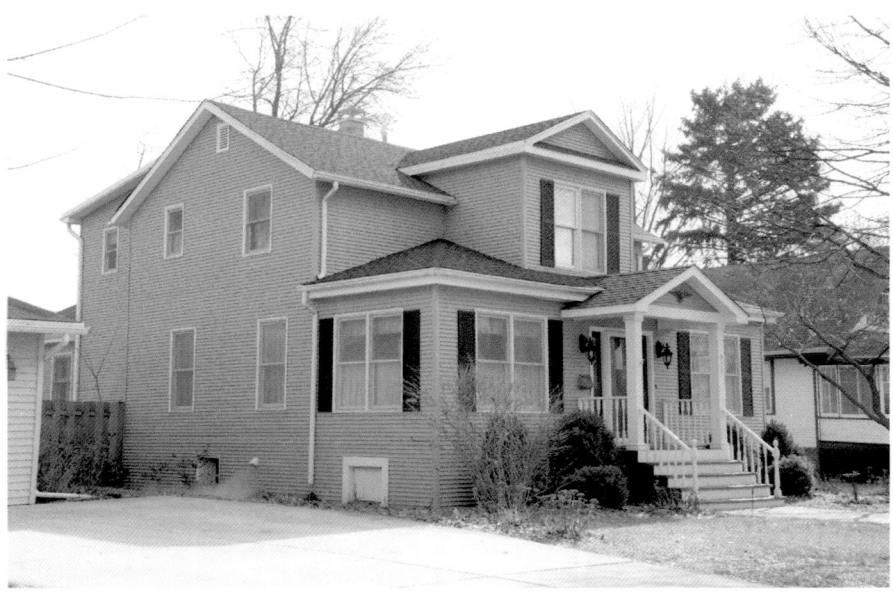

This home, at 925 North Dunton, was originally located at 101 West Davis, where it served as a municipal building from 1893 to 1913. *Photo by Gerry Souter.*

present with their cameras. They were rewarded with what could only move a true historian. Mickey Horndasch remembers, "When they tore down the outside aluminum siding, it fell away and revealed the inner white clapboard walls—the way the building looked when it was a little school." It was a real "Awwwww" moment for the community preservationists.[50]

Churches were forever rumbling through town and swinging around corners as populations grew and religious demographics shifted. One example stands out. In 1860, the Universalist church was built on the corner of Vail Avenue and St. James Street. St. Peter's Lutheran Church bought it in 1866 and moved it to 407 North Vail Avenue. In 1882, the building was rolled over to 308 North Highland, next door to the new Lutheran church, and converted into a parochial school. In 1889, this gypsy construction project was levered up from its foundation one last time and transported to its present location of 402–404 North Chestnut Street, where it was converted into apartments.[51]

While the Lutherans, Methodists, Presbyterians and Catholics (they shipped their church by rail to Des Plaines, Illinois) were busy tying up traffic with ambulatory architecture, the railroad was transplanting depots. The first depot built for the Illinois & Wisconsin Railroad in 1854 was hauled down to the south side of the tracks to diminished respectability as a freight shed. In its place a very nice station was erected in 1892 fronting onto Railroad Park, a landscaped area of trees, walks, benches and green lawn that gave a bucolic air to the business district. In 1930, the old 1854 station/freight shed was torn down to allow the laying of a third mainline track. The 1892 station was chipped away over the years until it was torn down in 1976 for a pseudo-colonial station complete with white pillars and a little steeple on the roof. By then, Railroad Park had vanished in a flood of concrete and asphalt to create a commuter parking lot.

While the transplanting of buildings fell out of fashion, the saga of the train depots had yet to play itself out. But for Tom Seibert, the end of the home-on-the-run took some of the adventure from his daily commute.

"I am sure this is not a complete list of all the buildings that have moved through Arlington Heights' history," he wrote. "It is enough to keep me watching my rear-view mirror. By the way, the house that blocked my driveway is currently behaving itself and rests quietly at the southwest corner of Arlington Heights Road and Oakton Street."[52]

Sadly, the "tear-down" has replaced the rambling residence. The wrecker's ball and the backhoe have leveled landmarks and eyesores alike. Off-loading from their flatbed transportation can strike fear into a neighborhood. However, their gouging and shattering destruction have also been tools of progress. They sit alongside dump trucks, road graders, street sweepers, street rollers and other heavy equipment in the inventory needed by Arlington Heights Department of Public Works. Supplemented by an army of subcontractors, these village workers keep up with busy developers, new construction, snow removal and the flow of water to and sewage from every building and residence.

Since the nineteenth century, the village has had to cope with constant growth in population, transportation, habitation and corporation. Nature, in its whimsical way, has always been the great leveler when it comes to progress. While Arlington Heights is located on a fairly well-drained plain, it was crisscrossed by a number of creeks that followed the low contours of the land. Though builders filled in some of these meandering waterways, gravity and hydraulics continued their relentless work, causing the streams to bubble to the surface to become mud. The downtown business district had a major headache when it came to keeping pace with the ooze liberally leavened with horse manure, cow pies and chicken droppings. All the buildings were raised four feet from their original foundations and iron stairs were constructed to the doorways.

People digging new holes to shift their outhouses often hit water, and rainy days frequently sent creeks rushing through ceramic pipelines under the

Construction and Destruction Go Hand in Hand

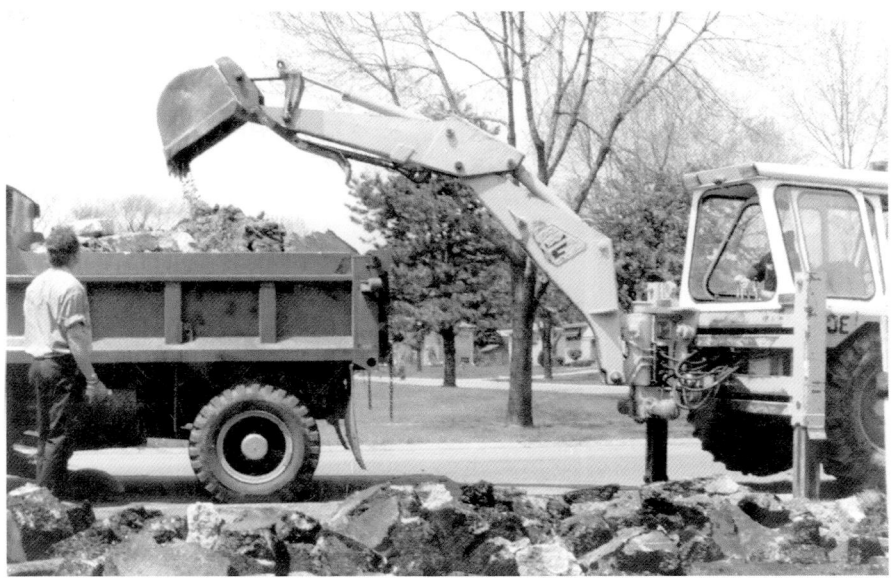

A backhoe, 1970s. Together with street rollers and bulldozers, these tools chewed up miles of old village pavement and knocked down walls. *Courtesy of Arlington Heights Public Works.*

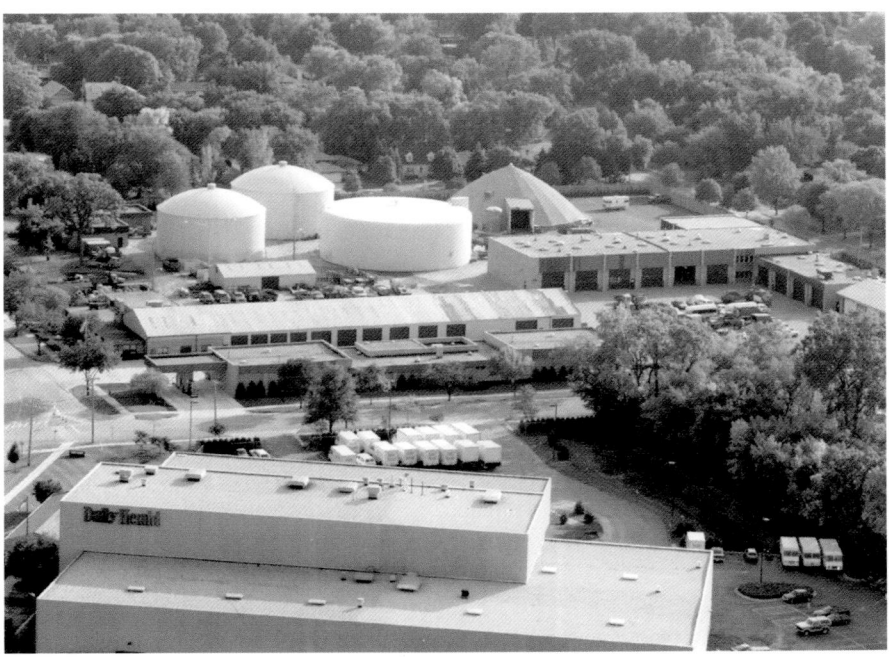

An aerial view of the public works building, 1988–89. *Courtesy of Arlington Heights Public Works.*

railroad tracks. A proliferation of septic fields threatened the drinking water from the wells dug on individual properties and later in communities. Huge steam-powered ditch diggers worked overtime as iron water pipes and brick sewers snaked beneath the clay soil.

Transportation by street and road became especially rigorous as the village grew, spreading out with annexations of contiguous properties. In winter, mud was replaced by snow—sometimes lots of snow. Horses towed wooden wedge plows that cleared downtown streets until gas-powered trucks mounted steel plows and carried sand purchased by the boxcar, or hopper load, at trackside. Travel at night required lamps that improved from kerosene to gas mantels and finally electricity, requiring utility poles to be raised for the overhead wires that still feed many of the neighborhoods.

Wells served the village until 1985, when treated water was provided from Lake Michigan via the Evanston Treatment plant. Sanitary sewage gathered by the village system was finally directed to the Metropolitan Water Reclamation District, which has treatment plants in nearby Skokie, Des Plaines and Schaumburg, Illinois. Tunnel sections reaching 35 feet in diameter were carved out of limestone rock 240 to 350 feet below ground to hold and move one billion gallons of water. Eventually, millions of gallons of storm water and wastewater will be stored in reservoirs and then treated and released into surface rivers and canals. This Deep Tunnel Project has gone

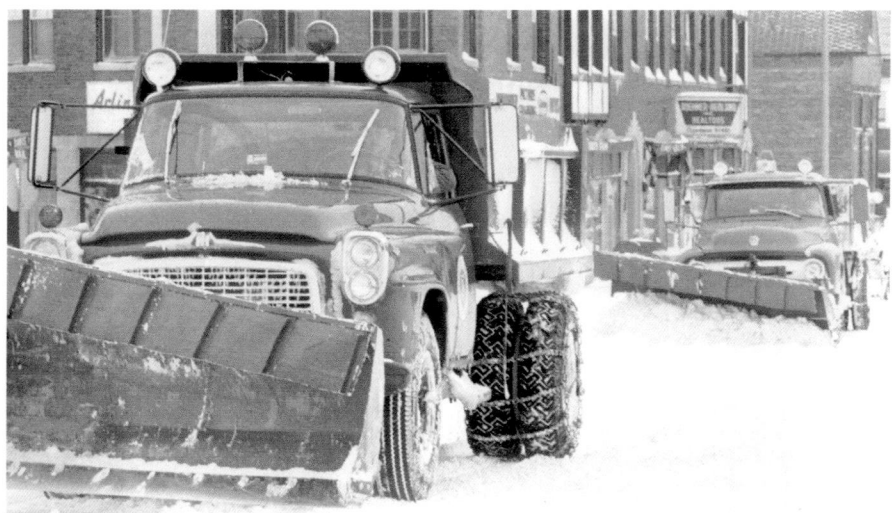

A snowplow struggling with the white stuff during the "big snow" of January 1967. *Courtesy of the Arlington Heights Planning Commission.*

Construction and Destruction Go Hand in Hand

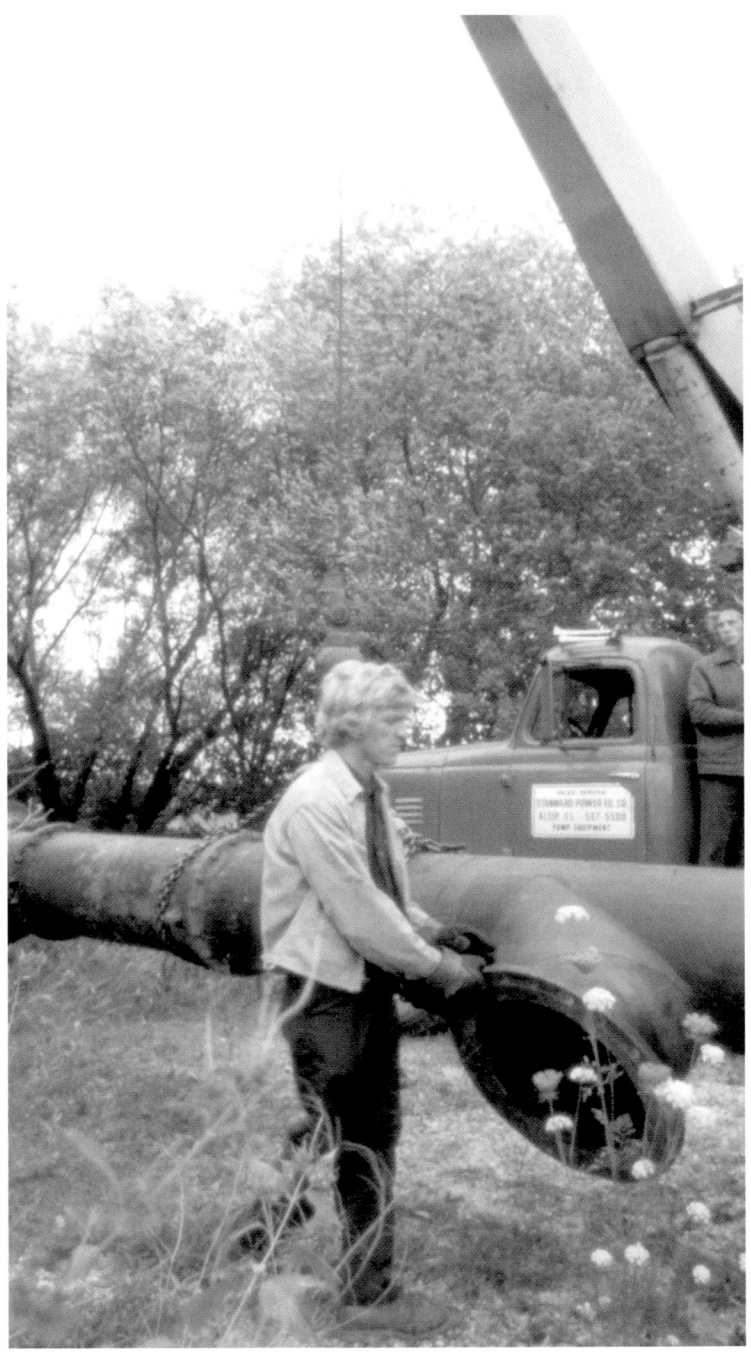

An iron pipe used in the Salt Creek project of storm water removal. *Courtesy of Arlington Heights Public Works.*

a long way to improving flood conditions in Arlington Heights and relieving stress on local sewers.

The growth spurt in the village during the 1970s and '80s that increased the strain on public utilities to keep up with construction and annexation had the opposite effect on public education. Following World War II came the baby boom and flood of returning GIs looking for fresh starts, a house, a car and a family. The tide of development swept into the suburbs. To meet the rising need for educating the young children, Arlington Heights experienced a school building program that expanded exponentially between 1950 and 1975. Almost every ballot during those years had an increased tax referendum to match the perceived growth.

Arlington Heights had completed the transformation from farm town to "bedroom community," where the majority of residents lived in the village but commuted to jobs elsewhere. It also became a community where young couples bought their first home, raised their families and then moved on to more upscale towns to the north and along the north shore of Lake Michigan.

The 1960s saw the introduction of the birth control pill and a change in roles as women began to leave the home for careers. The Vietnam War had polarized the country from 1965 to 1973, and more young adults chose to experiment with alternative lifestyles and "drop out" of the mainstream habits their parents had established. From 1974 to 1976, the United States experienced a staggering recession, adding to the uncertainties begun with the assassinations of President John F. Kennedy, his brother Robert and Martin Luther King Jr. in the 1960s. In 1974, OPEC (Organization of Petroleum Exporting Countries) raised crude oil prices 400 percent and gas pumps went dry across the country. That same year, President Richard Nixon resigned the presidency following the Watergate political scandal.

What had been the "normal" way of life seemed to vanish within the decade of the 1970s and then persisted with the "Me" generation into the 1980s and '90s. During this adjustment, school populations plummeted. Parents remained in their homes after their children grew up and left. Families had fewer children, and housing prices climbed beyond the reach of families with small children. Across School Districts 214 and 25, schools closed or were turned into administration headquarters. More children had to be bussed and strained budgets had to be relieved.

The most heart-wrenching example of this decline was the closing of Arlington Heights's first high school, which had graduated its first class back in 1923. Arlington High School existed because of women getting the vote and fighting for higher education in the growing village. The school had

Construction and Destruction Go Hand in Hand

become a fixture, a tradition in the community with its academic excellence, its Cardinal teams and the annual Homecoming Parade event. By the 1980s, plunging enrollments required closing two high schools, and despite legal battles, Arlington shut its doors in 1984, to be followed by Forest View High School in 1986. For years after the closing, former students continued to march behind the Arlington High School banner in the annual Fourth of July Parade.[53]

Symbolic as it was of the changes that were taking place in Arlington Heights, the July Fourth Parade also masked the glaring weakness that was becoming more evident each year. Every manner of social organization paraded through the village streets, from the Boy Scouts and Indian Princesses to the Lions and American Legion. The village orchestra played while riding on a flatbed truck. Floats from the Memorial Library and the Hickory Nuts rolled along behind the police department motorcycles, fire department ladder trucks and ambulances and the ranks of patriotic flag carriers. High school bands boomed and crashed and red fez–wearing Shriners zipped about in their midget automobiles. Everyone waved. Kids caught candy tossed by the marchers, and when it was done, the baseball fields over behind Recreation Park had been turned into Frontier Days, a three-day fun fest for the entire village. And through it all, the downtown business district baked stagnant in the summer sun.

Chapter 13

ARLINGTON HEIGHTS REINVENTS ITSELF

The sleepy farm town on the railroad tracks really began to sow the seeds for future growth in the early 1960s. Under the leadership of village president John G. Woods, Arlington Heights executed a number of high-growth-potential annexations. At the time, the village appeared to be an insatiable octopus, snatching up whatever unincorporated parcels it could gather. In fact, Woods turned out to be a canny administrator and secured a considerable portion of future development with an expanding tax base. Jack Siegel, the Arlington Heights Village attorney, remembered that hectic time:

> *In the spring of 1961 John was elected village president. John saw that things were going to happen here. The toll road had come in; O'Hare was spreading and obviously Arlington Heights could no longer be a sleepy cow town.*
>
> *We annexed everything in sight. Sometimes we had to race to the courthouse to get there before some other community.*

In 1963, a 400-acre plot bounded by Wilke, Dundee and Arlington Heights Roads was annexed for manufacturing expansion. The following year, 350 acres south of the village within the borders of Golf, Meier and Arlington Heights Roads were attached for commercial businesses. In 1966, 200 acres north of Dundee Road, containing two gravel pits and a trash pile that would become Nickol Knoll Golf Course, took Arlington Heights's boundaries clear to the edge of Lake County. On the heels of that annexation, Chesterfield Builders proposed to create 1,400 homes valued at $50 million on 345 acres north of the village. When it was completed in 1967, an additional 26 acres were tacked on for schools and parks. A drainage project became the 5-

Arlington Heights, Illinois

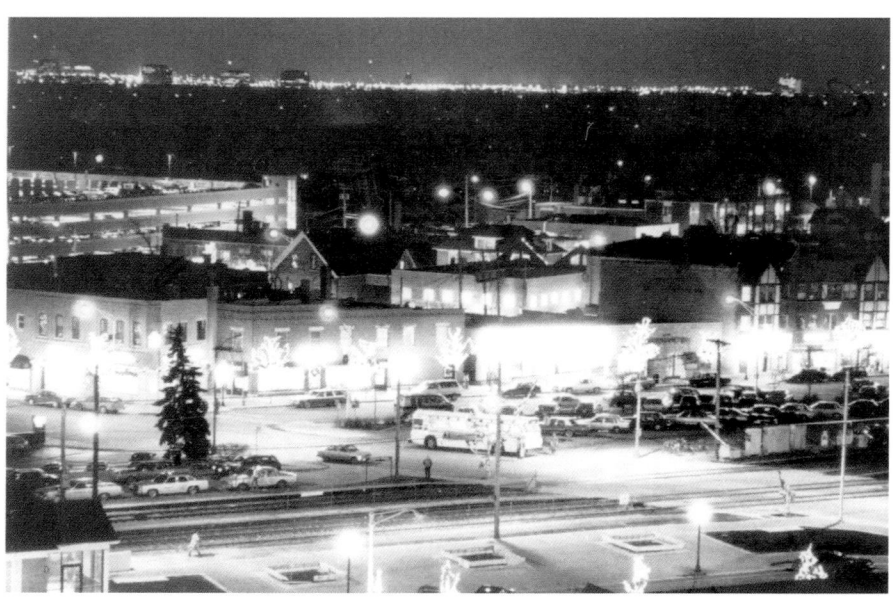

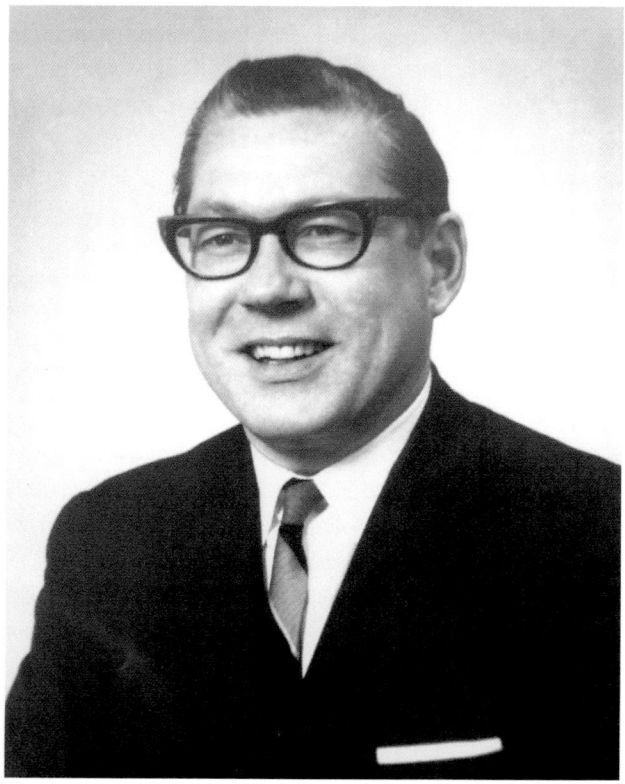

Above: A nighttime view of downtown Arlington Heights, 1980s. *Courtesy of Arlington Heights Public Works.*

Left: John G. Woods served as mayor from 1961 to 1969. His vision of a downtown revitalization wasn't realized until the late 1980s. *Courtesy of the Village of Arlington Heights.*

Arlington Heights Reinvents Itself

acre, man-made Lake Arlington, complete with boathouse, sailboat rentals, a dock and a paved walking path that encircles the recreation facility. Its water offers stocked bass, bluegill, crappie and catfish for anglers on a strictly enforced catch and release program.

According to Bell Savings reports, Arlington had issued 556 building permits for single-family residences from January 1964 through the end of November. The closest suburb, Oak Lawn, had issued nearly 100 fewer permits. In addition, village building commissioner Harold C. Best pointed out that building valuations on the more than 500 homes ranged from $20,000 to $60,000—with an average sale price of approximately $32,500.[54]

While the new acquisitions surrounding downtown Arlington Heights were virtual beehives of activity, if people who had lived in William Dunton's Section 29 land parcel visited the town in 1970, they would have felt right at home. There were the same street names, the same rows of small shops, the tracks and the station, the banks and even a few of the same names above the doors. Sure, the auto dealerships were now on Northwest Highway and the town dump was now a mall with two supermarkets, a bank, an appliance store and a hardware store, but otherwise, not much had changed.

While home developments added to the village head count, the services—water, waste disposal, fire and police protection—offset the additional taxes each home provided. According to Harold Best, the commercial properties paid the freight for the building boom. "The plan commission and village board have made it possible," Best said, "to accept, immediately, almost any desirable industrial or commercial project."

The declining central business district, for which new zoning had been approved to allow high-rise construction, had already brought some rough plans across Best's desk. He expected a high-rise apartment ring around the business center to begin developing in the late 1960s.[55]

The big malls in surrounding communities met the needs of the town's two-car families. The population aged during the 1970s and parked cars downtown were sparse on Saturdays—big shopping day. Downtown Arlington Heights came alive in the morning when the commuters left and in the evening when they returned. Between those times, a desultory snooze settled over the streets and shops. It was the same up and down the tracks; Mount Prospect, Des Plaines and Barrington, it seemed as if all the communities along the tracks had gone into hibernation. As mentioned earlier, world and national events had taken the wind out of everyone's sails as the 1970s stumbled along. Taxpayers were left in no mood to fund apartment buildings or blocks of the recent high-rise condominiums gaining favor in urban areas.

Arlington Heights, Illinois

Many Arlington Heights residents did not want to lose the character of their small-town atmosphere. To placate downtown merchants, a beautification project was launched in the 1980s. Decorative brick sidewalks were laid. The main streets were resurfaced, curbs were fixed and benches were placed to aid weary shoppers. Color-keyed awnings shaded shop fronts, adding a unity to the mix of small businesses. Green lawn spaces were carved out of the concrete and attempts were made to landscape the area that had been bulldozed away from what was once Railroad Park. The *Clock Tower* by sculptor Joe Burlini became a downtown landmark. To offer increased vehicle parking, brick and concrete three-tiered garages were erected like bunkers at strategic locations. Whenever high-rise apartments or condo plans were submitted to add more residential space to the downtown area, the plans were dismissed on two fronts. Few services downtown supported high-rise living, and members of a group calling itself the Shadow Project feared that their property values would plummet from being "overshadowed" by the tall buildings.

However, the inevitable could no longer be postponed. By 1986, on the north side of the tracks, Dunton Tower Condominiums rose as the first downtown high-rise. A year later, 200 Arlington Place lifted its steel and concrete skeleton. Up and down the railroad tracks, neighboring communities huffed and puffed about Arlington Heights breaking the skyscraper barrier and selling out to urban overcrowding and congestion. In 1993, Arlene Mulder was elected mayor and what had begun as an experiment in high-rise living space atop old Piety Hill suddenly discovered its enduring engine in TIF financing.

By 1997, Arlington Heights boasted 3,300,000 square feet of retail space and 7,043,700 square feet of office and industrial businesses. The village was spread along seven miles of prime suburban property values and was home to four major shopping plazas. And still, the prime core of the downtown business district remained virtually stagnant. TIF financing is a tool that uses future gains in taxes to finance debt to pay for projects that would otherwise be unaffordable to communities. Improvements generate higher tax revenues over time due to the increase in value of the real estate surrounding the improvement. These incremental tax increases occur within a specific area or "district." Arlington Heights leveraged this financial tool to literally explode the downtown business district into a national award-winning renaissance.

The backhoes and bulldozers went to work and the former sleepy wide space on the railroad tracks seemed cloaked in a perpetual cloud of plaster and brick dust. Many old buildings and homes were razed and residents bemoaned the

Arlington Heights Reinvents Itself

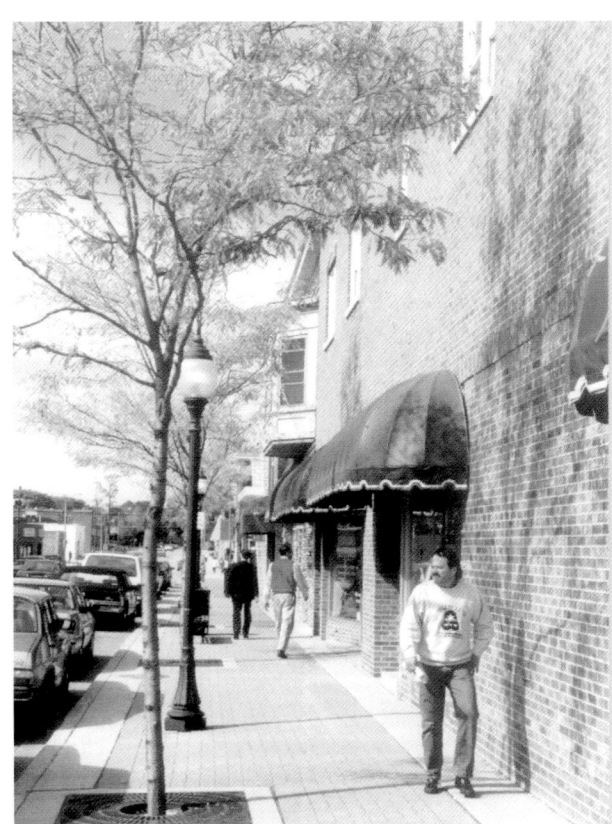

Right: Vail Avenue following upgrades in the late 1980s. *Courtesy of the Arlington Heights Planning Commission.*

Below: Curb repair, Davis Street, 1980s. *Courtesy of the Arlington Heights Planning Commission.*

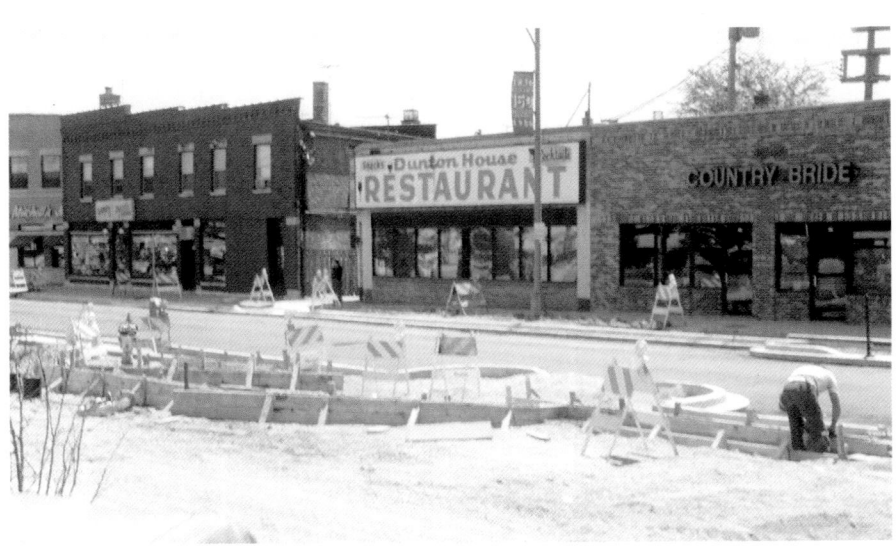

Arlington Heights, Illinois

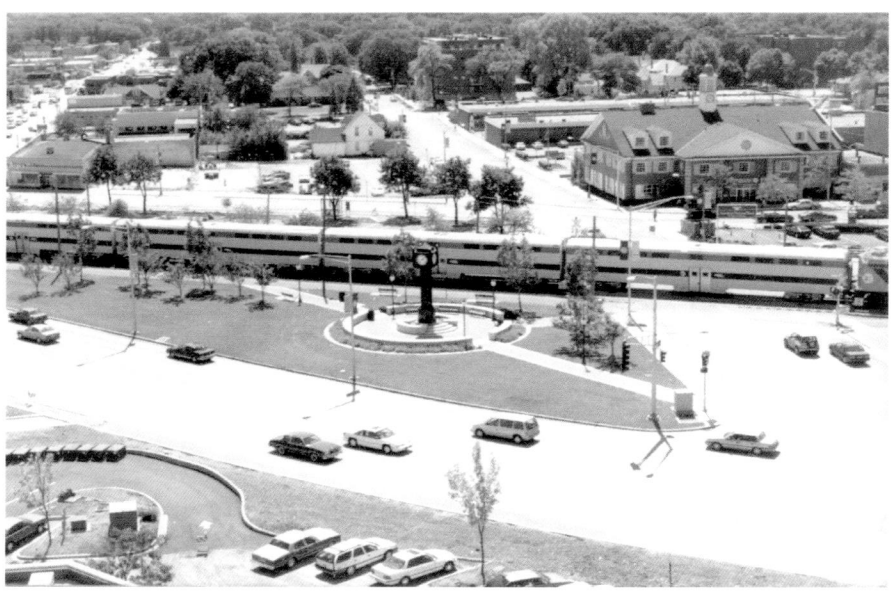

An aerial view of the clock tower square, 1988, about ten years prior to the construction of Arlington Town Square. *Courtesy of Arlington Heights Public Works.*

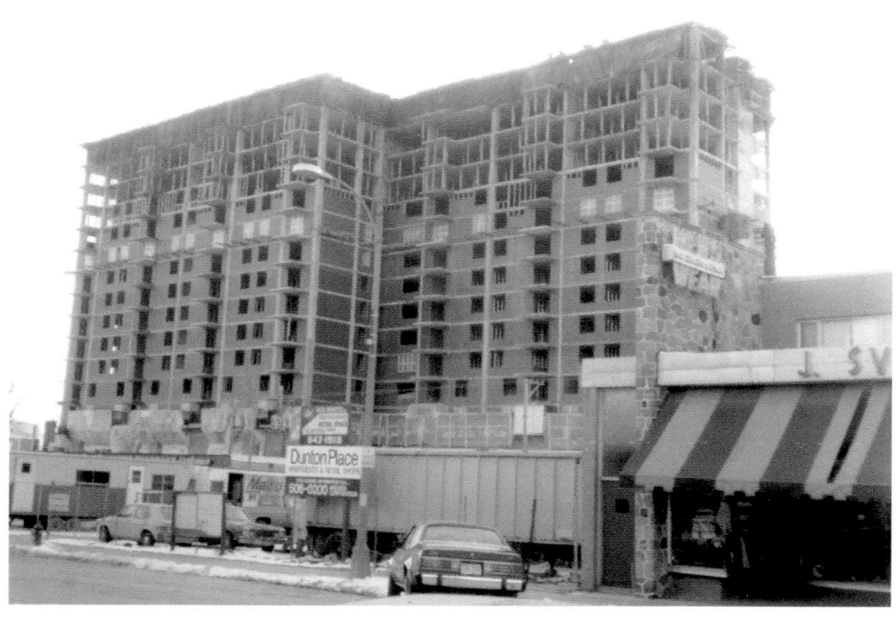

Dunton Tower construction, south of Campbell Street, 1986. This was the first high-rise built in the village. *Courtesy of Phil Theis.*

Arlington Heights Reinvents Itself

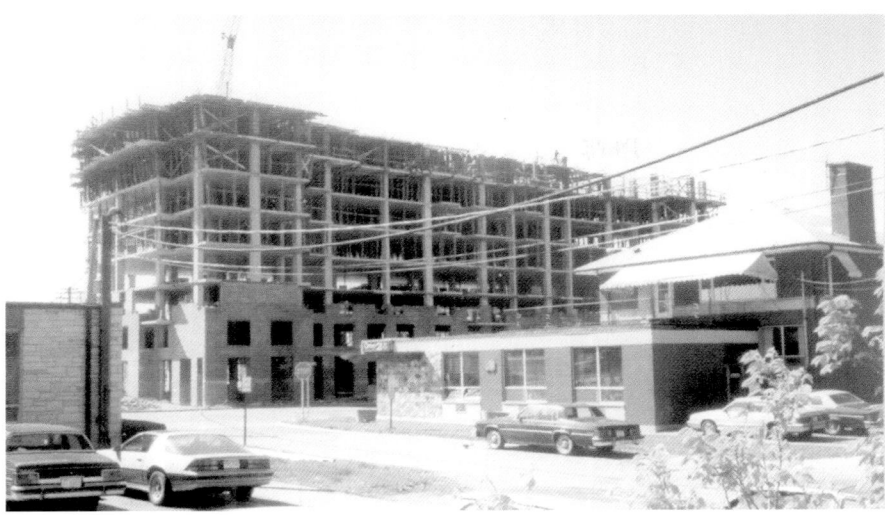

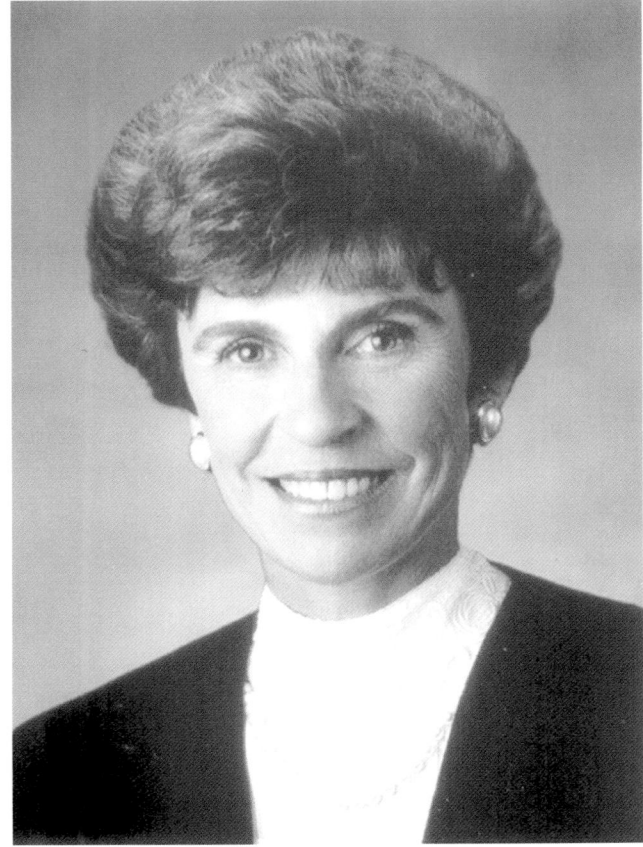

Above: Construction of 200 Arlington Place, 1987. *Courtesy of Phil Theis.*

Right: Arlene Mulder, mayor of Arlington Heights since 1993. *Courtesy of Arlene Mulder.*

Arlington Heights, Illinois

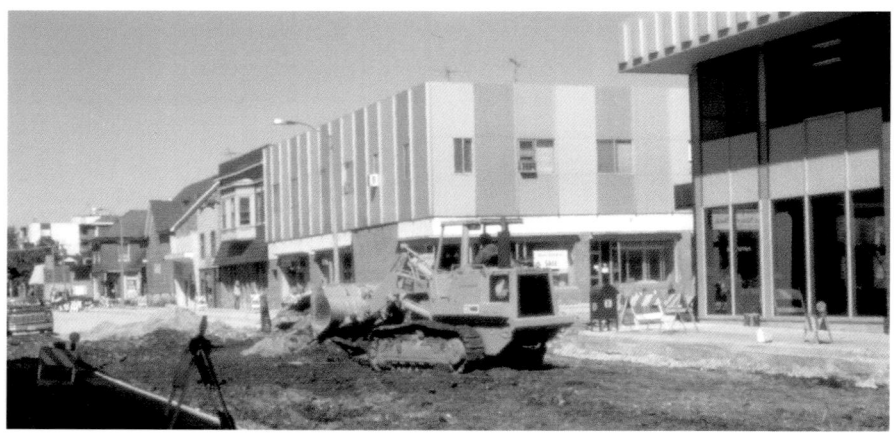

Campbell Street resurfacing, 1980s. This was the beginning of a series of improvements in the downtown business district. *Courtesy of the Arlington Heights Planning Commission.*

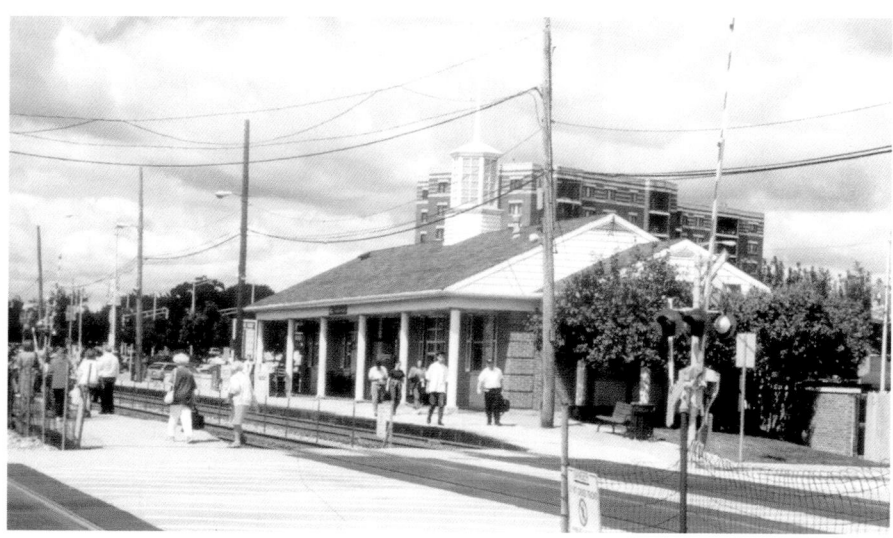

Train station, 1980s. The station was built in 1976. *Courtesy of the Arlington Heights Planning Commission.*

loss of familiar landmarks. Davis Street disappeared from Arlington Heights Road to Evergreen. The 1976 train station was rolled into a pile of rubble. The Countryside Restaurant crashed down in a shower of bricks. Small shop owners who could no longer pay the increasing rents and taxes shut their doors. Village board meetings became shouting matches as the steelwork climbed into the sky.

Arlington Heights Reinvents Itself

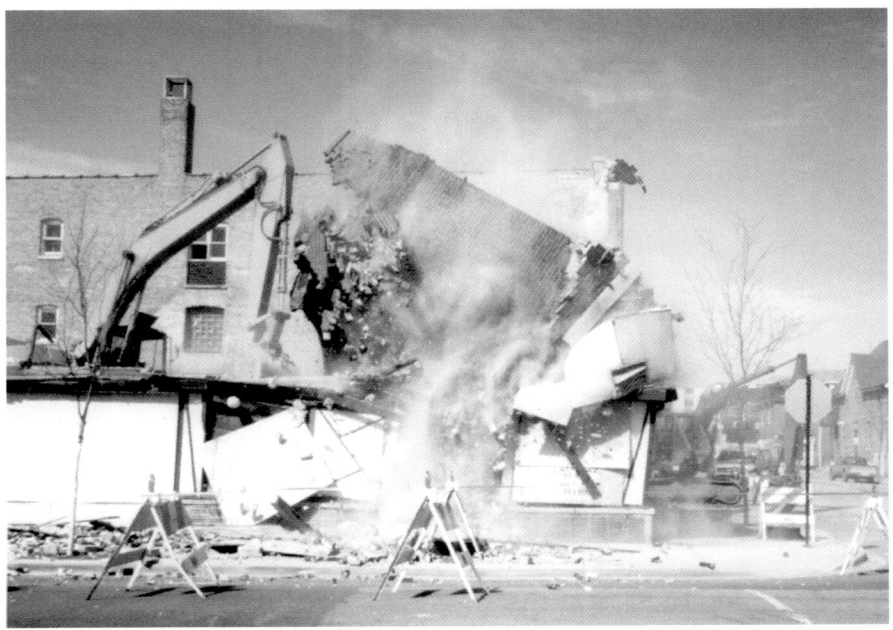

Demolition of the Countryside Restaurant, Campbell Street and Dunton Avenue. *Courtesy of Phil Theis.*

And then the new train station was dedicated, a graceful, copper-clad remembrance of the 1892 beauty that once sat in Railroad Park. Its gabled roof and cobbled walks set off the brick and brown wood exterior. Its lines echoed the Tudor Vail-Davis building across the street that survived from 1928. A Jewel food store that had replaced the former two-story village hall and town bandstand had a face-lift and expansion to match its neighbors. Shopping at the Jewel were the new residents of the imposing Village Green Condominiums that rose up on Vail Avenue, with commercial businesses filling their street-side floor.

On the area bounded by Arlington Heights Road, Sigwalt, Evergreen and the tracks, the new Arlington Town Square Plaza launched its shops and restaurants, anchored by the new Arlington Theater movie complex and a Starbucks Coffee Shop above spacious underground parking. Behind the theater loomed the Town Square Condominiums, rising twelve stories above a commercial business base.

Campbell Street wore a new look, with a mix of landmark buildings such as the Hagenbring corner block, but it also boasted the town's latest entertainment venue, the Metropolis Performing Arts Centre. This facility,

Arlington Heights, Illinois

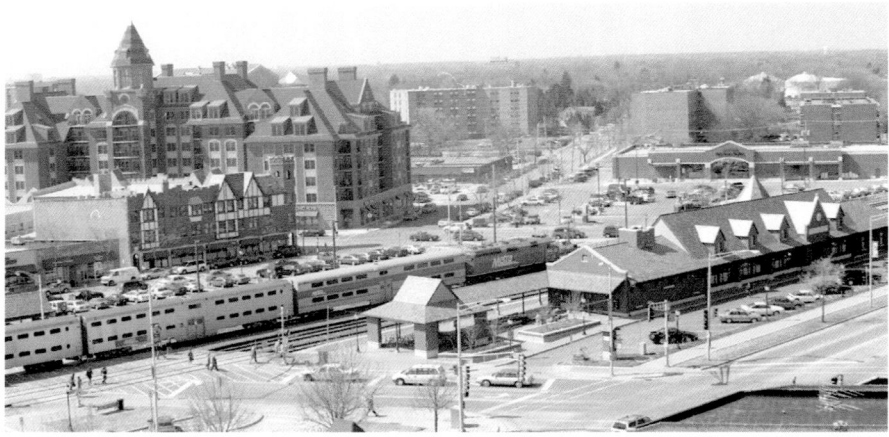

A view of downtown Arlington Heights, 2001. The building to the left with the turret is the Village Green condominium, restaurant and retail complex. *Photo by Gerry Souter.*

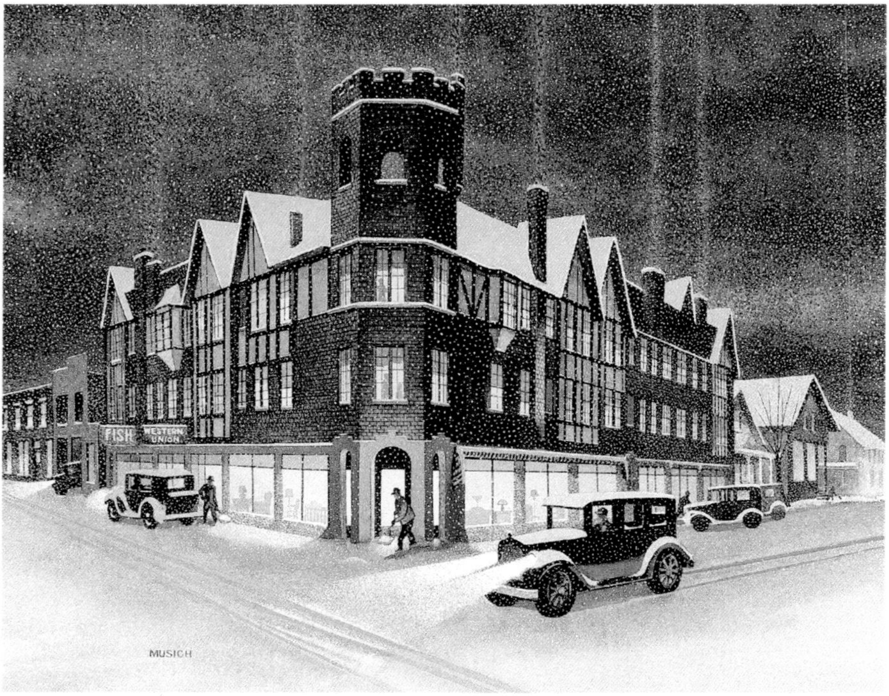

Vail Davis Building, 1928s. This Tudor architecture was in vogue during the village's building boom in the 1920s. *Painting by Jack Musich.*

Arlington Heights Reinvents Itself

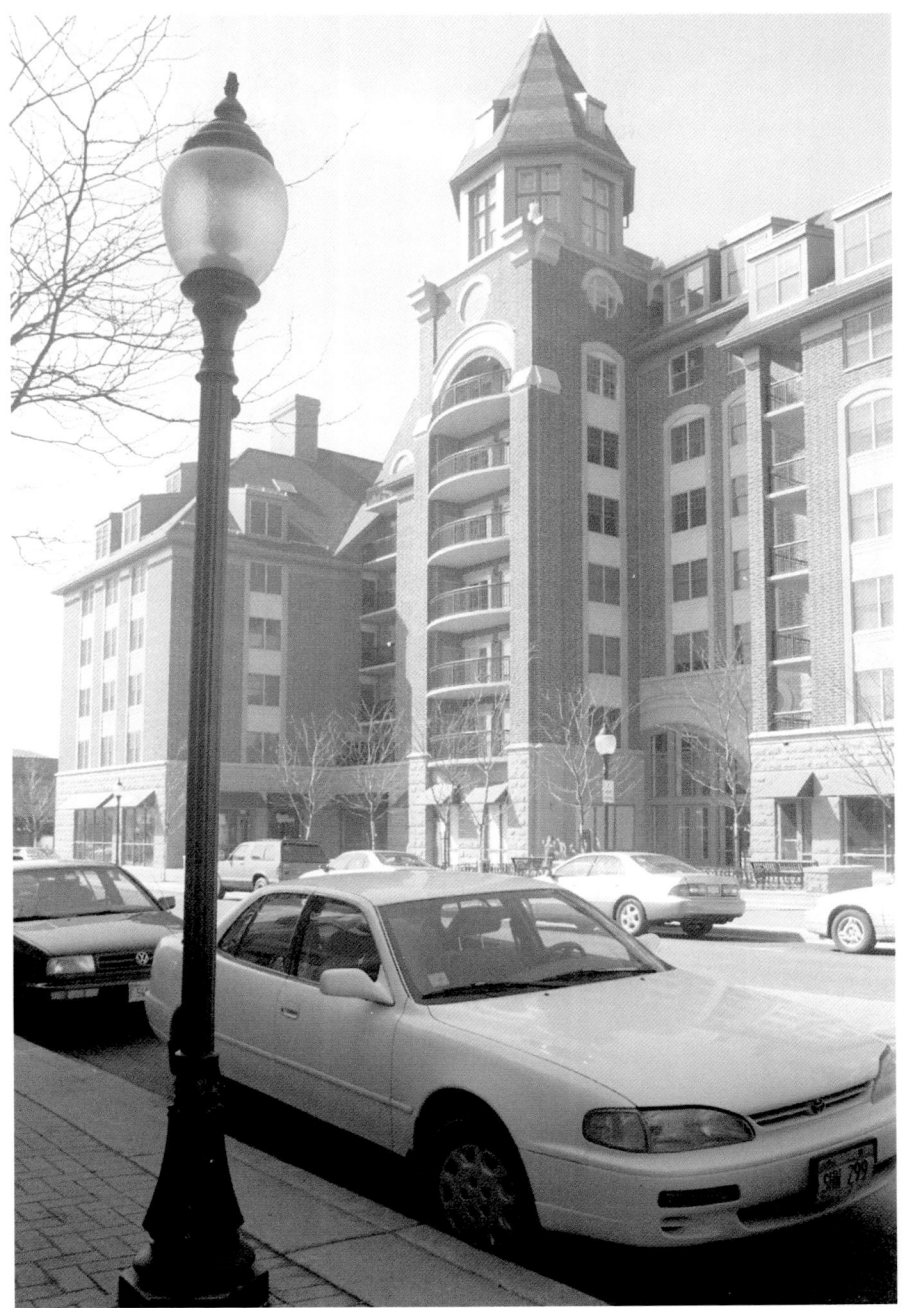

Village Green entrance on Vail Avenue, 2001. *Photo by Gerry Souter.*

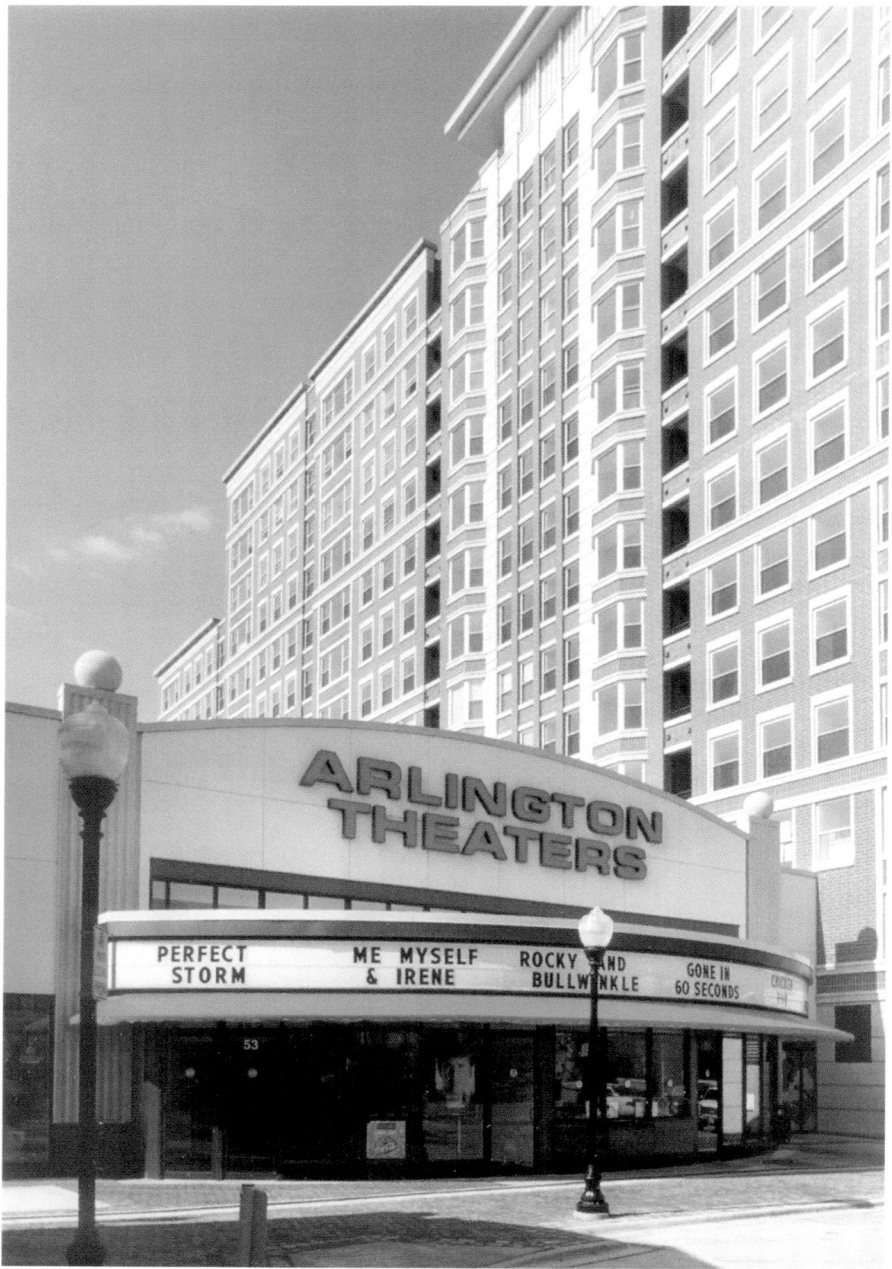

By 2001, Arlington Heights once again could boast of a movie theater. This is part of the Arlington Town Square complex. *Courtesy of Joseph Freed & Associates.*

Arlington Heights Reinvents Itself

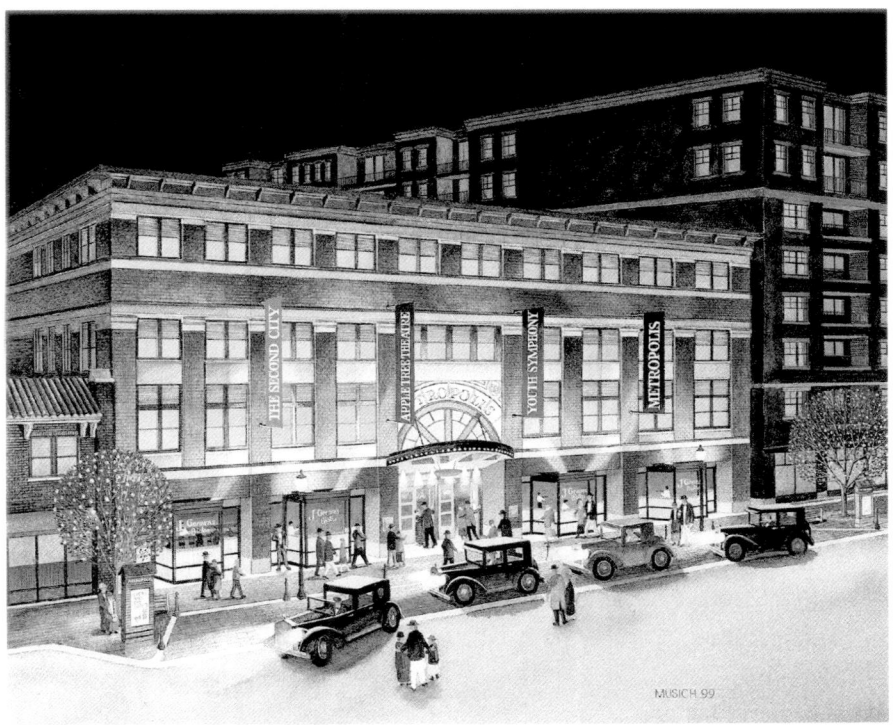

The Metropolis Performing Arts Centre. *Painting by Jack Musich.*

with its main stage and floors of music and dance studios, is a creative hive of continually changing performances. More high-rise residential buildings followed down Vail Avenue while low-rise town houses complemented the south side of the village, forming a transition into the tree-lined neighborhoods beyond.

The '90s saw yet another threat to what residents recognized as the stability of village neighborhoods. Banks and lenders began offering adjustable rate mortgages (ARMs) to potential home buyers. These loans offered a much lower repayment schedule that could be adjusted upward later, tied to the increased value of the home. ARMs allowed home buyers to purchase much more expensive homes than they might have been able to afford with the higher fixed-rate mortgages. Developers and contractors began buying up small, older houses, scraping them off the property and shoe-horning large six- and seven-figure homes onto the original lot. These huge mansions dwarfed the older homes that remained on the block, seriously affecting the scale of the neighborhood.

Arlington Heights, Illinois

Houses began to sell as tear-downs and the oversized homes stuffed into small lots proliferated. In 2007, aroused neighborhoods made their voices heard, and the suitability of these mansions became a sticking point with the village. By 2008, however, many of these big houses stood empty as home values declined. Soon, many homes were worth less than their upwardly adjusting mortgages and owners defaulted on payments. As 2009 arrived, across the nation, homes spiraled down in value, causing banks to foreclose and personal bankruptcies to rise sharply, which caused a downturn in the global economy.

But what happened with the "loss of old-time charm and friendliness" that longtime residents feared? From spring to fall, the downtown—both north and south of the tracks—is filled with the sound of music. Free concerts are offered in Harmony Park at Vail and Campbell Streets and on the huge tree-shaded lawn that is North Park in the center of Piety Hill, flanked by the namesake's churches. Both locations are alive with the splash of large decorative fountains with a music all their own. Neighbors bring canvas and tubular chairs, buy snacks at the nearby eateries and swap gossip with friends. The character of each venue is different. In town, the music caroms off the rising walls of architecture and the sidewalks are busy as condo and neighborhood residents mingle, passing by the grassy patch where guitar riffs alternate with dulcimer tinkling, rising up to balconies and the still wings of circling sparrow hawks. At North Park, the trees rustle and chortling water cascades over carved stone. The music of chorales and chants, or violins and Elvis, gets tangled in the branches.

At the start of each racing season, the town's international landmark, Arlington Park Racecourse, holds its "Mane Event"—a street fair filled with food, tents and music ranging from rock to romantic. Just east of downtown, Frontier Days continues its more than thirty years of midway and concert entertainment over five days each summer, beginning with July Fourth and the big parade.

The downtown is alive again. In the Chicago newspapers, Arlington Heights is known as "a restaurant town" where every manner of food from tapas to sushi, served in thirty-three establishments, can be had with the appropriate wine. Outdoor sculpture surprises strollers and the exiting theater crowd passes through winners from a day at the track. Summer breezes waft around top-down vintage automobiles driven by gray-headed men with their sweethearts at their side. It's a night for cruising.

The scale of Arlington Heights's new downtown revival is complemented by its latest structures. The 1960 village hall on Sigwalt Street has been replaced by the John G. Woods Campus, which houses the services of the

Arlington Heights Reinvents Itself

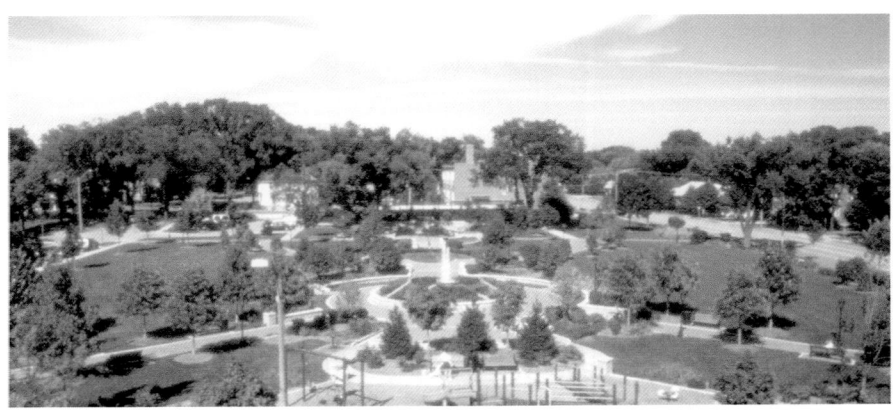

A view of North School Park, looking north. The Virgil Horath fountain is in the center. The site was donated to the community by William Dunton with the stipulation that it always remain open land. *Helen Horath estate.*

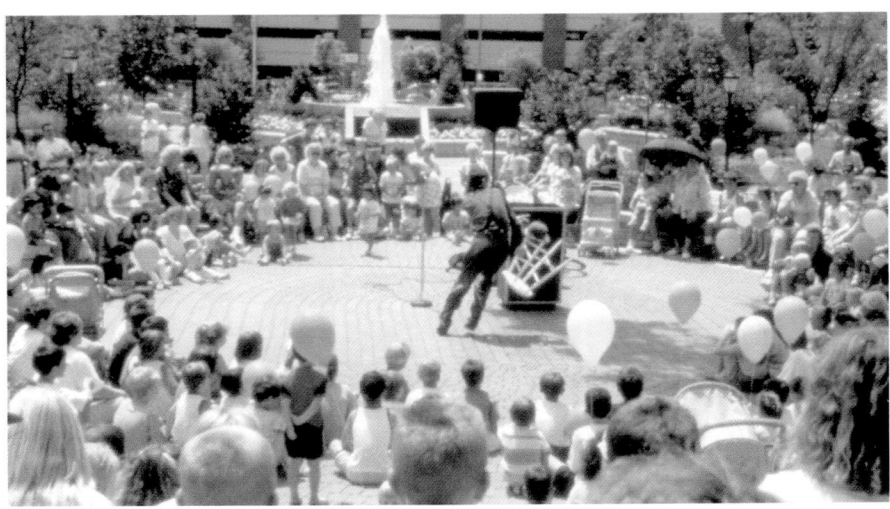

Entertainment at North School Park. The park is the site of events such as the annual Christmas tree lighting ceremony, the Autumn Fest, Art in the Park exhibit and entertainment throughout the summer. *Courtesy of Arlington Heights Public Works.*

Arlington Heights, Illinois

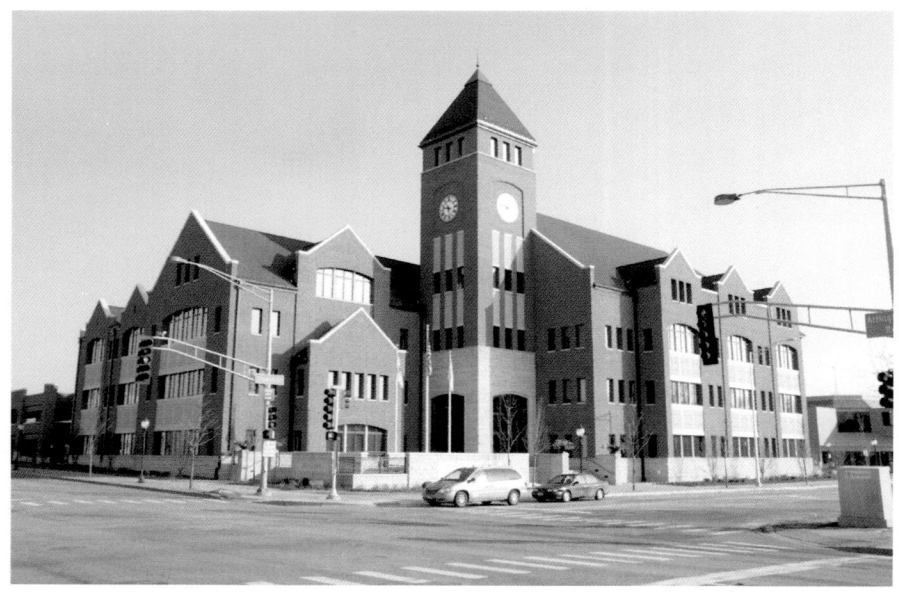

The John G. Woods Municipal Campus, completed in 2008. *Photo by Gerry Souter.*

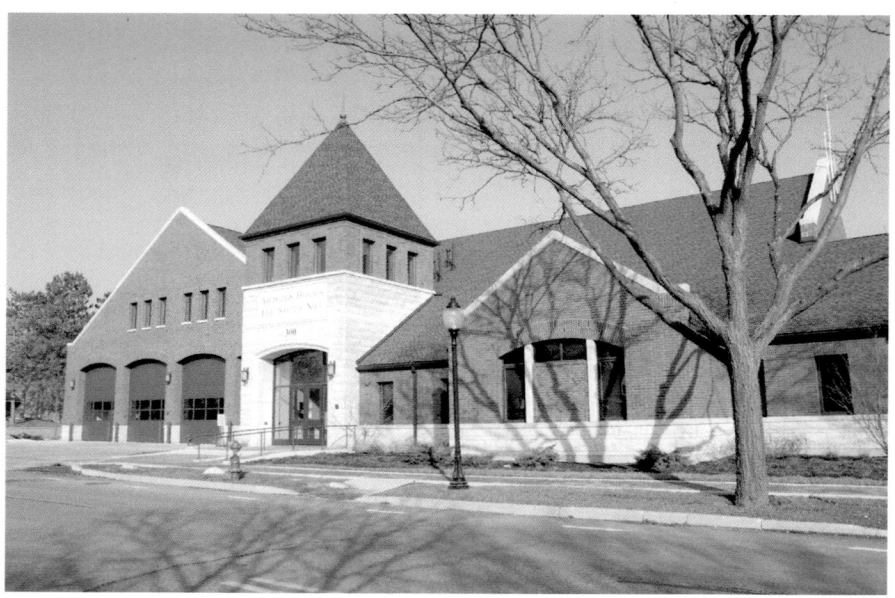

The new village fire station, part of the John G. Woods Municipal campus. *Photo by Gerry Souter.*

Arlington Heights Reinvents Itself

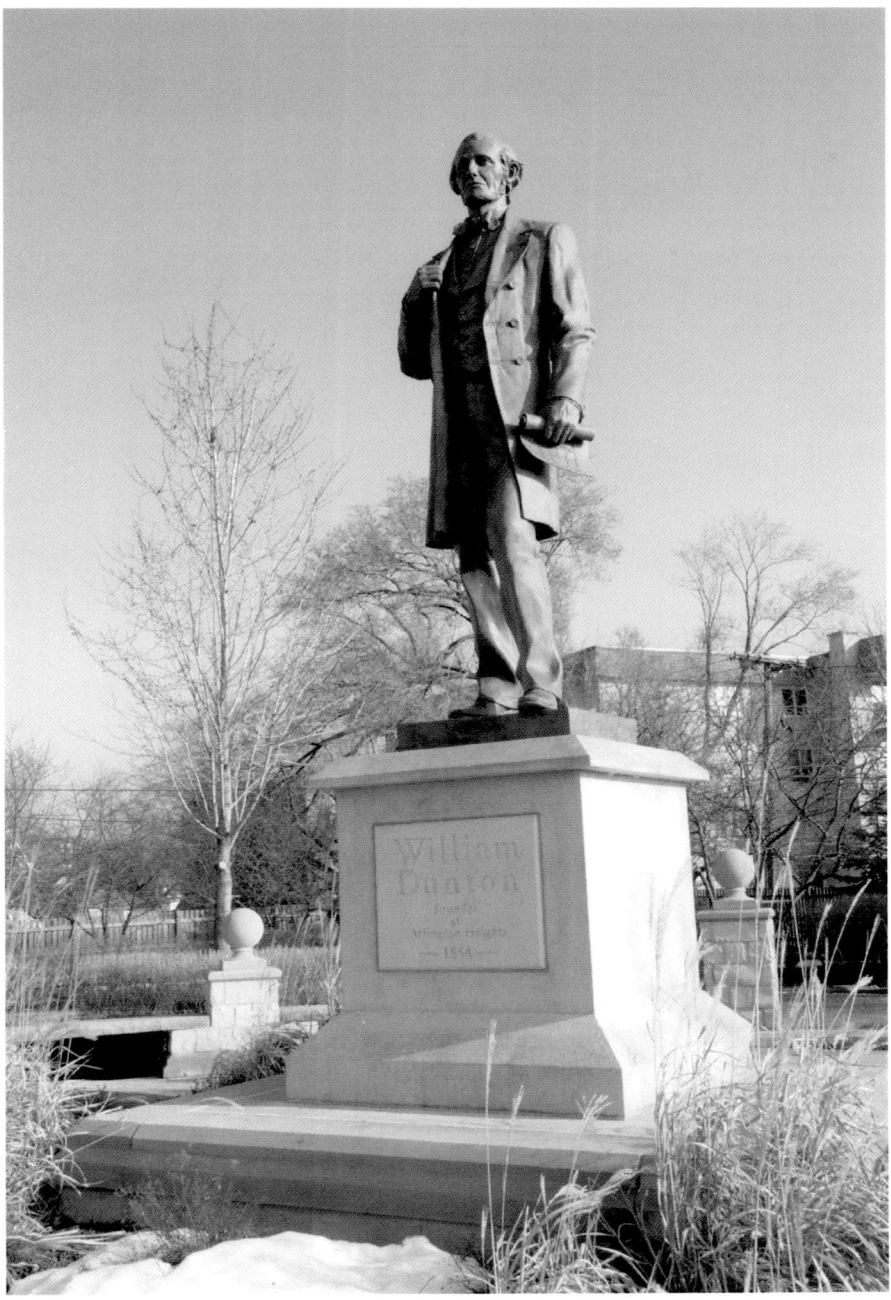

A statue of William Dunton by local sculptor Fran Volz, Northwest Highway and Arlington Heights Road. Dunton's first home was moved near this spot when the railroad came through. *Photo by Gerry Souter.*

Arlington Heights, Illinois

village municipal government and joins the police department and a new fire department, altogether referred to by winking residents as the "Taj MaHall." Facing this imposing edifice stands a bronze sculpture of William Dunton, gazing across the (now Union Pacific Railroad) tracks from a small park near the corner of Arlington Heights Road and Northwest Highway. This is about where his home came to rest after it was moved from where the railroad surveyed its tracks through his living room back in 1854. As his wife wrote back then, there was just their little house in the midst of the vast grass prairie that rippled like waves to the distant tree groves.

Chapter 14

NO CONCLUSION IN SIGHT

This story comes to an end, but Arlington Heights's growth and prosperity show no signs of conclusion. The village has come so far since young Bill Dunton drove that first stake into Section 29 on the windswept prairie. What did Frederick Miner think about after stacking the last of his goods on shelves of West Wheeling's first trading post and looking out his front door at wagons heaped with families and belongings rolling along the Pottawatomie trail that became Arlington Heights Road? Did the hardware drummers who stepped off the Illinois & Wisconsin Railroad car onto the Dunton station platform with their sample cases see any future in the cluster of trackside shops? Or did they just see the Union Hotel sign and think of a cold beer to wash the soot from their throats?

And what do the amazing people who contributed stories and photographs and revealing facts to this book think about their decades spent here? Some see their names on street signs. Others read their names in the accomplishments of great-grandchildren and on the rows of marble markers left by generations past. Arlington Heights, for all its progress and feats of rebirth, is still a small town in the fabric of the nation. But in that smallness lies its greatest strength, which binds it into a place called home.

NOTES

CHAPTER 1
1. Robinson and Moore, *History of Illinois*, 71.
2. Margot Stimely, "Early Illinois Territory," in *Chronicle of a Prairie Town*, 17.
3. Chicago Title and Trust Company, Abstract of Title, 1117690, William H. Dunton and wife.
4. Jim Montgomery and Barbara Bell, "Educating the Kids: The Education Evolution in the Village," in *Chronicle of a Prairie Town*, 217.
5. Kansas City Star, Midwest Voices, *They Only Had an Eighth Grade Education*, http://voices.kansascity.com/node/3416
6. Stimely, "Early Illinois Territory," in *Chronicle of a Prairie Town*, 16.
7. Professor Gerhard Rempel, "The Revolution of 1848" (Western New England College). http://mars.wnec.edu/~grempel/courses/wc2/lectures/rev1848.html.

CHAPTER 2
8. Michael Winkels letter, 1844, collection of Janet L. (Winkels) Souter.
9. Gerry Souter, "Our Railroad: Growing Up By the Tracks," in *Chronicle of a Prairie Town*, 20–21.
10. Margery Frisbie, "A Third Place," *Daily Herald*, January 30, 2000.
11. *Chicago Tribune*, March–June 1863.
12. *Charles Sigwalt Civil War Diary*.
13. Fred A. Vance, "Remembrance from his father, an original settler of Dunton and an friend of William Dunton." Recorded November 5, 1943. Arlington Heights Historical Society Archives.
14. Myrtle Lauterburg, interview by Margery Frisbie.

15. James Murray, Lauterburg and Oehler, interview by Janet Souter, February 2009.
16. Eileen O. Daday, "Our Village in Newsprint," in *Chronicle of a Prairie Town*, 100–03.

Chapter 3
17. Tom Seibert, "From the Ground Up: Architecture of Arlington Heights," in *Chronicle of a Prairie Town*, 208–12.

Chapter 4
18. Daniels, *Prairieville USA*, 159.
19. Dave Mills, "Arlington Heights Fire Department—The First Ones on the Scene," in *Chronicle of a Prairie Town*, 67.
20. Margery Frisbie, "Memories of the First Law Enforcement," *Daily Herald*, May 14, 2000.
21. Margery Frisbie, "Cranking Memories of Old Car Days," *Daily Herald*, October 8, 2000.
22. Daniels, *Prairieville USA*, 137.
23. Ibid., 138–39.
24. Ibid., 137–39.

Chapter 5
25. *Cook County Herald*, August 15, 1917.

Chapter 6
26. Souter, "Our Railroad," *Chronicle of a Prairie Town*, 26–27.
27. LeVern Gieseke, interview by Janet Souter, February 2009.
28. Tom Gaughan, "What Makes Arlington Park Run?" in *Chronicle of a Prairie Town*, 90–95.

Chapter 7
29. Dolores Bokelman, interview by Janet Souter, February 2009.
30. Shirley Brown, interview by Janet Souter, January 10, 2009.
31. Ann Loughery, *Everybody Has a Story—Memories of Arlington Heights*, 2002, 91; Donna Dattilo memoir and interview, January 2009.
32. Bob Frisk, interview by Janet Souter, January 23, 2009.

Chapter 8

33. Douglas Aircraft Company, Inc. advertisement, *Arlington Heights Herald*, July 21, 1944, 9.
34. Gerry Souter, *Time and Time Again*, interview with Carl Weinrich. Arlington Heights Historical Society promotional film, 1997.
35. World War II Rationing, www.ameshistoricalsociety.org/exhibits/events/rationing.htm.
36. Daniels, *Prairieville USA*, 249.
37. Ibid., 251.
38. Gerry Souter, "Village at the Home Front," in *Chronicle of a Prairie Town*, 88.

Chapter 9

39. *NPGS Newsletter*, Nike Preservation Group, Inc.
40. Dr. Robert Muench, memoir to the author, January 2009.
41. www.grazian-archive.com/governing/kalos/Kalos_P02_C04.html.
42. Bill Kruser and Robert Loerzel, "The American Dream: A Post-war Building Boom," in *Chronicle of a Prairie Town*, 139–47.

Chapter 10

43. Pat Gieseke Winkelman, interview by Janet Souter, January 29, 2009.
44. John Brouhard, "Few Flaws…Part of History," *Arlington Cardinal Newsletter*, Spring 1983.
45. Souter, "Growing Up By the Tracks," in *Chronicle of a Prairie Town*, 27–29.

Chapter 11

46. Mills, "Arlington Heights Fire Department," in *Chronicle of a Prairie Town*, 70–71.
47. Irene Larson, "Police Department: To Better Serve the Community," in *Chronicle of a Prairie Town*, 187–91.
48. Beth Willwerth, "America's 'Noble Experiment' Comes to Town," in *Chronicle of a Prairie Town*, 126–127.
49. Gaughan, "What Makes Arlington Park Run?" in *Chronicle of a Prairie Town*, 97–98.

Chapter 12

50. Interview with Mickey Horndasch, curator, Arlington Heights Historical Society, 2009.

51. Seibert, "From the Ground Up," in *Chronicle of a Prairie Town*.
52. Ibid.
53. Montgomery and Bell, "Educating the Kids," in *Chronicle of a Prairie Town*.

CHAPTER 13

54. Kruser and Loerzel, "The American Dream," in *Chronicle of a Prairie Town*.
55. *Arlington Heights Herald*, "Arlington Hts. Is Suburb Building Leader," December 31, 1964.

BIBLIOGRAPHY

Arlington Heights Herald

Charles Sigwalt Civil War Diary. Arlington Heights Historical Society.

Chronicle of a Prairie Town. N.p.: Arlington Heights Historical Society, 1997.

Daniels, Daisy Paddock. *Prairieville USA.* N.p.: Historical Society and Museum of Arlington Heights, 1971.

DigitalPast. North Suburban Library System, digitization initiative featuring local history collections from cultural institutions. www.digitalpast.org.

Frisbie, Margery. *Daily Herald.*

Kansas City Star, http://voices.kansascity.com/node/

Library of Congress Online Catalogue.

Loughery, Ann. *Everybody Has a Story—Memories of Arlington Heights.* N.p.: 2002.

National Archives (NARA).

Robinson, L.E., and Irving Moore. *History of Illinois.* New York: American Book Company, 1909.

Souter, Janet, and Gerry Souter. *Arlington Heights, Illinois, Downtown Renaissance.* Charleston, SC: Arcadia Publishing, 2001.

ABOUT THE AUTHORS

Gerry and Janet Souter are full-time authors who have lived in Arlington Heights, Illinois, for thirty-eight years and raised their three children to adulthood there. They bring to this text the experience that comes from writing forty-two books for mainstream publishers since 1997. This history is compiled from stories told by longtime residents who have seen Arlington Heights grow from a sleepy farm town to a vibrant, award-winning community. Their tales are mixed with the historical highlights that measure that growth. Having traveled throughout the world, represented by agents in New York and California and with publishers in Paris and London, the Souters return constantly to their roots, their neighbors and the charming village they call home.

ABOUT THE ARTIST

Jack Musich is an Arlington Heights resident and noted Illinois artist. He studied art at the Layton Art School in Milwaukee, Wisconsin. His work won a scholarship to the Rochester Institute of Technology in New York. Jack operated his own commercial art studio for thirty years, gradually moving into fine art expressions. His historic paintings and commissions are recognized and coveted throughout the midwestern United States.

*Visit us at
www.historypress.net*

This title is also available as an e-book